T0209214

A NEW BREED OF SHARK

Become a Fierce & Fearless Female Entrepreneur

WRITTEN BY
MOM, WIFE, CEO

CHARLIE FUSCO

authorHOUSE®

AuthorHouse™
1663 Liberty Drive
Bloomington, IN 47403
www.authorhouse.com
Phone: 1 (800) 839-8640

*The author has made every effort to ensure the accuracy of the information within this book
was correct at the time of publication. The author does not assume and hereby disclaims
any liability to any party for any loss, damage, or disruption caused by errors or omissions,
whether such errors or omissions result from accident, negligence, or any other cause.*

Published by AuthorHouse 9/7/2016

ISBN: 978-1-5246-2369-2 (sc)
ISBN: 978-1-5246-2370-8 (hc)
ISBN: 978-1-5246-2371-5 (e)

Library of Congress Control Number: 2016908251

Print information available on the last page.

*Any people depicted in stock imagery provided by Thinkstock are models,
and such images are being used for illustrative purposes only.
Certain stock imagery © Thinkstock.*

This book is printed on acid-free paper.

*Because of the dynamic nature of the Internet, any web addresses or links contained in
this book may have changed since publication and may no longer be valid. The views
expressed in this work are solely those of the author and do not necessarily reflect the
views of the publisher, and the publisher hereby disclaims any responsibility for them.*

*This book is available for bulk purchase at
www.thatgirlcharlie.com*

EARLY ENDORSEMENTS

"Charlie Fusco defines Female Entrepreneur - Together we've created infomercials, co-hosted a successful national radio show, appeared on stage together, and spent hours brainstorming strategies. Sassy, sexy and savvy - she just gets it! In her book she inspires and shares her secrets about being mom, being CEO, being wife and so much more - a unique perspective from a woman… named Charlie! A must read :)"
Forbes Riley, Celebrity TV Host | Creator of SpinGym

"Brains, Boobs, & Balls is definitely a page turner for women and men, but mor.e so it pushes you to turn the pages in your life. Grabbing you and your attention by the collar, Charlie delivers her story like no one else can, ripping you out of your comfort zone, pulling back the curtain on her journey, and inspiring you to take back control over yours."
Tanner Gers, CEO | ABSolutely Lean LLC

"Charlie Fusco has gotten it right! What a journey she has had. Her story is brutally candid, inspirational, and motivating. A fabulous read." **Kathy Murphy, President | Gray Consulting International Meetings & Incentives**

"Absolutely loved this book, what a perfect title! Incredible business insight from the trenches… done with love and laughs and no punches pulled. Thank you for writing this book Charlie, my wife is loving it too."
Jim Sweeny, President & Founder | honestonline.com

"A must read book for any one feeling lost or wallowing in self-pity! This book will pick you up & kick your ass into productivity mode. Fusco is an inspiration as she says, "Look for the Cinderella moments to create your own happily ever after." Get this book today! It will be a life changer to inspire you to be best-self in business, family, & the bedroom."
Karen Ognibene, Executive Editor | South Jersey MOM Magazine

EARLY ENDORSEMENTS

"I picked it up for the title and because a friend recommended it. As I started reading I thought it was a book geared towards women; however, Charlie quickly jumped into both personal stories and business lessons that apply to me and every one. Stories about courage, faith (being fearless), risk, and practical lessons you can apply to your own life. Focusing on the things you can control and not the negatives (happiness), hard work to overcome weaknesses, developing core drivers to help with decision making, practicing gratitude… lots of stories that offer a different perspective on ideas for success that other great motivators have talked about, like having no fall back plan and people who you would die for to help motivate… and the lessons go on and on. The book has plenty of humor, shock (Many times I asked myself if she really is using this story to teach the business lesson), and fun to keep you turning pages as well."
Craig Handley, CEO | ListenTrust

"Who wouldn't read a book called Brains, Boobs, & Balls? Lol. Charlie Fusco is an absolute super star! She is smart, witty and is a powerhouse. Her content is based on real world experiences and as a fellow women entrepreneur I absolutely resonate with her. I started my own business six years ago. I had a dream of selling my own content, my own information products online. I can't tell you how many people told me over the years that I was wasting my time and that I should just let it go. They just didn't see my vision. But I ignored all the naysayers and with a little brains, boobs and balls (of my own) - I can proudly say that I've taught tens of thousands of consumer products companies across the globe on the subject of selling to retailers. So I highly recommend Charlie's book because it is magical!"
Karen Waksman, Founder and CEO | Retail MBA

EARLY ENDORSEMENTS

"Right at the outset, what attracted me to this book was the title, not the content. That's probably because I am an old guy who got through the business world the old fashioned way – hard work, kissing butt, and ducking low while the boss was in the neighborhood. That penchant, though, I confess, was because I was ill-equipped when it came to Suave, Sophistication, or Seductive traits found attractive to those rare women with whom I came in contact with in the business world. Which is a long way to say that I was attracted to this book much as opposite poles of a magnet are attracted… This book does indeed have some hilarious passages. It is not, though, a book of humor. The author has an engaging style of communication that also is steeped in common sense. Much of her more pertinent advice stems from decisions she made as her business was shifting into that next level. A level in which she had not the self-confidence needed to weather her new challenges. To go into further detail would negate your need to read the book, so I shall stop here. Needless to say, though, this is a refreshingly interesting take on how to succeed in the business world for women – however, men should read it also, for much of the tips can be adapted."
Bill Anderson | Top 500 Amazon Reviewer

"Ms. Fusco is vulnerable and takes big risks in this entertaining and inspiring book! She intimately shares some of her darkest moments, while keeping you laughing and appreciating the honesty and candor she revels. This is a must read for any woman entrepreneur! I thoroughly enjoyed the advice and funny real life moments that she graciously shared."
Natalie Hale, CEO/FOUNDER | Media Partners Worldwide

EARLY ENDORSEMENTS

"Charlie's book is a hands on guide showing how to go for what you dream. Her often funny, always blunt, intelligent and practical advice on how to succeed in the business world as a woman, wife, partner, mother, CEO, etc. is truly a must read for any woman who wants to do more with her life. Men will also enjoy her comments since it is written as a commentary on what she has done, didn't do, should have done and is doing now to make her dream of being a CEO of her own company work for her and her family. Charlie presents 17 lessons, starting with her explanation of Brains, Boobs and Balls (some of her funniest stories), through her lesson on Core Drivers (my personal favorite), her concept of the 3Ps, Play, Passion and Progress, a lesson on Compartmentalizing (which all woman do to survive), and other valuable ideas."
Denise Healy, Corporate Research & Intelligence | Independence Blue Cross

"The book subtitle aims itself at entrepreneurs, but I submit that audience is too self-limiting. This book is for ANY person who dares venture into the business world, male or female, young or old, rich or poor. And for those of us on the later side of life, it is a fantastic way to vindicate ourselves on our own "failing up" while simultaneously releasing us to laugh at ourselves and know "we are not alone" in the crazy ways we've lived our lives and followed our passions."
Mary Ellen Himes, VP/SR Trial Counsel | Fidelity National Law Group

"Being a woman in the business world is tough. Once in a while, you stumble upon advice that you find yourself putting into practice daily. I'm so happy that I found this book. It is an honest and insightful guide for people to use as they navigate through entrepreneurship. From heartbreak to labor pains, Charlie shows you how to bring together everydaylife and business so that both can be the star. Play, Passion, and Progress - I will use those words every day going forward."
Jodie Riccelli, COO | Exponent Entertainment

EARLY ENDORSEMENTS

"This book isn't just for women entrepreneurs. This book is for anyone who wants to learn about business from someone who has done it and is doing it. Her stories I found funny, honest and insightful. I enjoyed and would recommend."
Michael Alden, Esq., Author of *Ask More Get More* and *5% More*

"I bought a private vocational school in 2010. I brought it back from the brink of extinction by sheer determination, guts and well, Brains, Boobs and Balls. I overheard recently that the previous owner said the school would grow more if I "didn't travel so much, or if I put in electric paper towel dispensers." Mind you, I've opened my second location and am getting ready to open location number three. I feel the need to justify my actions to him - but then just let it go because it's none of his business anymore. The lessons I've learned and adopted since buying the school through interaction with people like Charlie Fusco will far surpass even my wildest dreams. Being a female entrepreneur requires brains, boobs and balls every day!"
Shari Aldrich, President | Bodymechanics Corporation

"While I am not prone to reading books these days with social media platforms and the never ending barrage of e-mails, I actually read Charlie Fusco's book. I started, prepared to put it down quickly, and go one with my day. To my surprise, I didn't. I ended up reading the entire book in one evening. My take away is that anyone can gain a lot from watching Charlie battle through from virtually the ground floor to becoming one of the most respected producers in the business. Her take no prisoners attitude resonated with me. Page 187 stood out but then again, who wouldn't like reading about themselves. Regardless, this is a 5 thumbs up book! Buy it now!"
Evan B. Morgenstein, CEO & Sport Agent | CelebExperts and PMG Sports

EARLY ENDORSEMENTS

"Fusco's unsentimental voice in telling the stories of her battles to become successful is immensely winning (writing about her early days as a businesswoman juggling a family life, she quips that her office was "the room off my living room, and it was fully equipped with a desk, computer, phone, fax and crib"). Her willingness to own her fallibility is refreshing in a genre that often touts complete certainty. Why, even men could learn a thing or two here. A brash, unconventional, and often deeply personal battle cry for rejuvenating female entrepreneurs in the workplace."
Kirkus Review

INTRODUCTION

IMPORTANT
DO NOT SKIP THIS SECTION

The week of July 11th, 2016 marked the official release of **Brains, Boobs, & Balls: Life Lessons Any Female Entrepreneur Can Follow**. Perhaps you are one of the thousands that picked up a copy during the seven-day period of my first solo book launch. Or maybe, you are one of the people who would have never bought a copy because the title of the book was… offensive. More likely, you have no idea what I am talking about. Let me explain.

To most authors, the thought of selling enough books to make it to the Wall Street Journal Best Seller List is a dream. I certainly never even considered making the New York Times Best Seller List or any others for that matter. That didn't stop me from spending seven days refreshing Amazon.com and tracking the rankings of my book like a mother hen counting her chicks. Amazon is arguably the biggest source for tracking book purchases that is used to create these best seller lists. I was careful, however, not to count my chicks before they officially hatched.

On that Saturday, I woke up to *Brains, Boobs, & Balls* having the following ranking:

Amazon Best Sellers Rank:
#1 in Kindle Store > Kindle eBooks > Business & Money
#1 in Books > Business & Money
#2 in Kindle Store > Kindle eBooks > Nonfiction
#12 Paid in Kindle Store overall

On that Sunday, I had calls, emails, and texts from my publisher, other online book stores managers, book marketers, and a couple of previous Best Selling authors — all congratulating me because they were certain I would land somewhere firmly on the Wall Street Journal Best Seller List the following Thursday. If you're a non-fiction author, especially one that writes business books, a spot on the WSJ list means more speaking gigs, higher consulting rates, higher visibility, and an enhanced reputation.

On Thursday, my assistant was refreshing the Wall Street Journal page every five minutes waiting for the list to update. But before the list went live around 4:30PM, I received the following email from my book marketing team that set in motion a chain of events that led you not to be reading ***Brains, Boobs, & Balls: Life Lessons Any Female Entrepreneur Can Follow,*** but instead ***A New Breed of Shark: Become a Fierce & Fearless Female Entrepreneur.*** Is it the same book? Almost. Here is the email chain:

> Thu, Jul 21, 2016 at 4:17 PM
> "Charlie, I have bad news. The (Wall Street Journal) list just refreshed and we did not make it. We sold far more than the books at the bottom 5 on the list and probably should be #4 on the list. I'm contacting the WSJ for an explanation why."

After a few phone calls, my book marketing team was informed why I had not made the list.

> On Thu, Jul 21, 2016 at 4:31 PM
> "Charlie, they're saying the title was too racy. Really?! Ugh! We actually made it to #1 among all non-fiction ebooks on Saturday and #9 among all ebooks for the week."

I had no idea that a title could be too racy and get you excluded from the list, despite actual sales. I thought it was like selling Girl Scout Cookies – if you sell the most cookies, you get the big badge. But no, book selections are biased. Really? I asked him to please check again as it didn't make sense.

> On Thu, Jul 21, 2016 at 7:10 PM
> "Charlie, from what we tracked, the book should have hit at around #4. It was in the top 10 non-fiction for 4 days and #1 on some days. Other than a few books, the other top ten books were fleeting. They were titles that got a one day sales spike from Bookbub.com or eReadernews.com, etc and then disappeared from the top 10 the next day. The sales for your book were undeniable."

I asked my team to check for a number of sales that we could verify independently. Perhaps other books did sell more than mine! Let's be fair.

> On Thu, Jul 21, 2016 at 8:48 PM
> "Hello Charlie, We had more than enough sales numbers. It took approximately 4,000 sales to make the list. We exceeded that. We should have been in the top 5. The WSJ can arbitrarily pass on a book for title or cover. The final sales numbers reported to the list come from Nielsen. The book was not removed from [Nielsen]. The sales should have had it squarely in the top 5 for the week [on WSJ] but we were passed over."

So it's true? My title is too racy? I was passed over even though I sold thousands of copies more than books #6-10? I emailed my publishing/

distribution partner and asked just how many books they reported being sold.

> On Fri, Jul 22, 2016 at 12:02 PM
> "This is preliminary and this is what we got out of the system and the numbers will be finalized on the royalty statement. Month-to-date unit sales covering period 07/11/2016 to 07/20/2016 is 6093. We do not get the data from all the online stores until the end of the month. Below is only Amazon and does not include books sold on other sites like 800CeoReads, Hobo, or Barnes and Noble, those will come in the month end report."

I wasn't crushed by the news that I didn't make the Wall Street Journal list. I was one of many authors that week pushing my product out into the world. I sold 6,093 books on Amazon alone in one week? I thought that was actually AWESOME! I guess enough people were interested in the content behind the racy cover! I closed out the week as a Hot New Release on Amazon squarely between the new Harry Potter book and the new Clinton book. That's not too shabby. Clearly, our nation has a wide variety in taste when it comes to what is important to them.

There are many books that, despite never making the pages of the Best Seller lists, go on to sell thousands of copies and have a great fan base. In the end, content is king and book reviews and word of mouth build the kingdom. I've been a product marketer in the consumer space for more than twenty years and I fully understand that you have to be in it for the long game. I didn't write the book to be a best seller – I wrote it because women have been asking me for years for advice on being a 'fempreneur' and juggling a personal life too. I wanted to share my advice with them.

Yet, the fact was, I did FAIL at becoming a WSJ Best Selling Author the week of July 17th, 2016. My VERY RACY title and cover may never grace a Best Seller List, even if the content is not racy and can actually help people. Which made me wonder: *50 Shades of Grey* made all the Best Seller lists and the inside of *that* book is certainly racy, if not outright pornographic.

My staff who helped launch the book were outraged. My outside book marketing team was frustrated. The few colleagues and friends I shared the news with were astonished. My husband started laughing.

"That's so cool that your book is too racy for a newspaper's best seller list. There has to be some honor in NOT making the list because of that reason. What was too racy? The fact that you said Boobs? Balls? Or that they were in the same sentence as Brains?"

We both had a good chuckle because honestly neither of us could figure it out. If a woman curated the list, we weren't sure if she disapproved of the boobs or the balls or both. If it was a man, did he disapprove of balls being listed after boobs? Or was it the use of slang to describe the anatomy and I should have titled the book *Gray Matter, Soft Tissue, and Testicles!*

The truth is that no reason has no be provided.

If you are NOT one of the 6,000+ people who purchased the book in the first days it was available for sale, let me assure you the content inside has merit.

- I urge women to master Excel spreadsheets so they can better forecast their business, cash flow, and stay calm during financial crisis.
- I discuss how successful female entrepreneurs must acknowledge they are self-sabotaging their own business because they don't trust their own intelligence enough.
- I'm a huge teacher of self-care as being a major key to succeeding in business and at home.
- I cover the importance of having a wide access network.
- I detail the bankruptcy risk or better yet how to avoid it all together.
- I lay out specific strategies for making a woman a more powerful presenter in the boardroom so she can close deals faster and for more money.

- The book covers decision making.
- There is a formula included for birthing new ideas in business.
- I explain why women should ignore the glass ceiling and stop blaming men for the inequality in the workplace.
- The raciest part, I guess, is that that women should not to give up being passionate just to build successful business – this includes how they treat their partners and themselves in the bedroom.

Perhaps it was the title and cover that excluded me, websites where people purchased the book on, that didn't assign the same weight to make these lists. The reality could be I did not sell enough in the right channels. In any case, I got to thinking. What if I had marketed it differently?

If you've already read *Brains, Boobs, & Balls*, I would still encourage you to read *A New Breed of Shark* with this new insight in mind. Drop me a line at www.ThatGirlCharlie.com with your thoughts on this whole situation.

So how did I go from Boobs & Balls to Sharks? Simple! I asked one of my strategic partners, Evan Morgenstein, CEO of CelebExperts, what title he thought could replace *Brains, Boobs, & Balls* and still sell well while being true to the nature of the book?

Within moments, he came up with the title and gave me three reasons:

- The word 'shark' has become directly linked to product marketing thanks to the hit TV show *Shark Tank*. Product marketing is my business, I share the industry with them, and my life is not much different than what goes on behind the scenes of that show.
- Sharks are fierce and fearless and I preach that in the book already, just using different words.
- Women are not generally called sharks in business. It's a term reserved for successful (and sometimes ruthless) businessmen. I write about women maintaining their 'femininity' while still being killer in the boy's boardroom. I have become a new breed

of successful (and sometimes ruthless) businesswoman that travels in a pack rather than swimming alone.

I asked 40 people what they thought of the new title and 38 of them loved it. That settled the problem of coming up with a new name, which was good since I only had a week to turn it around in order to hit the September 1ˢᵗ re-release date.

So, why re-release my book under a new title and cover a mere 60 days later? If it's good enough for The Beatles, it's good enough for this girl!

In 1966, The Beatles released *Yesterday and Today*. It is perhaps the most famous recalled album cover of all time. Advance copies were sent to stores and DJs, generating an immediate uproar over the cover showing the band covered in baby parts and bloody meat. All copies were ordered to be returned to the manufacturer where they would be "pasted over" with a new cover and sent back to stores. Only a handful of copies escaped the "repasting" and are of course valuable collector items. Many people tried to peel the new cover off, making an original "unpeeled" copy valuable, too!

That same year, The Mamas and the Papas' *If You Can Believe Your Eyes and Ears* was forced to change the cover because apparently an unoccupied toilet was offensive. The original cover was quickly withdrawn and replaced with an awkward song-title box covering the offending bowl; eventually the entire bathroom was cropped out!

The list of artists with recalled album covers is long and distinguished, featuring:

- **Rolling Stones, *Beggars Banquet* (1968)**
- **Rod Stewart, *An Old Raincoat Won't Ever Let You Down* (1969)**
- **David Bowie, *The Man Who Sold the World* (1970)**

- **Michael Jackson, *Ben* (1972)**
- **U2, *Boy* (1980)**

You get the picture! Retitling a book is really no different than what these record companies did in order to get this legendary music out into the word. The difference in my situation is that you can still buy *Brains, Boobs, & Balls* <u>right now</u>, both online and in selected stores, and you will always be able to do so. But you can also buy *A New Breed of Shark*, and perhaps you'll feel better about leaving this version on the coffee table. The point is that my message will be available through whichever title and cover resonates with you more!

The other point that is important to understand is that making a Best Seller List does not make a book good or bad. NOT making the list because of an arbitrary decision that flies in the face of the modern belief that women should be seen equally in the media begs a response. Should women (or men) in business be worried about 'saying it like they feel it' for fear that they will not get to where they want to be? That's not a part of any reality I want to live in.

At the time of my writing this new introduction, I have no idea if *A New Breed of Shark* will make any of the Best Seller Lists the week it debuts. My team believes that we are better marketers for having FAILED to make the lists the first time and that we will make it this time. And if *A New Breed of Shark* makes the list, they are going to be sure to make it public knowledge that the same book that FAILED has now SUCCEEDED with only a title and cover change. I hope that inspires entrepreneurs, business owners, and those on the verge of birthing a new idea to find a new way to succeed when failure is staring you in the face. When you are told NO, turn right around and GO another direction until you get where you want to be.

Keep pushing through. Keep FAILING-UP to success. Make sure you always learn and apply the lessons in the FAIL.

So what have I learned by FAILING to be a Best Selling Author that I can share with my business clients, product marketers, aspiring entrepreneurs, inventors, and students of business?

Here are my Top 5 Take-Aways:

1. BOOKS *ARE* JUDGED BY THEIR COVER!

If you're trying to sell a product these days (book, services, supplement, skincare, kitchen gadget, etc) you MUST consider the packaging and the name of the product very carefully. It is not good enough that the name of your product is available as a .com, or that it gives your product standout qualities, or that it fits your overall brand. Nor is it good enough to just put together packaging without consideration for how it will be viewed – not only by the consumers, but by retail buyers, list compilers, and specialty retailers that you are banking on to sell your product. If my title was so offensive to a newspaper like the Wall Street Journal, do I have a prayer that a specialty retailer like Barnes & Noble would dare carry it in their store on an actual shelf? The potential scandal! Only time will tell. But if you plan to sell multi-channel, make sure your packaging will draw in your Amazon customers without it being passed by at Bed Bath & Beyond.

2. 3RD PARTY ENDORSEMENTS COUNT

Product reviews and word of mouth are great when it comes to selling your product or service – keep collecting them. But face the facts – consumers want 'legitimate proof' from a third party that your product/ service is worth it. Find out which third parties your customers count on in your business (AARP, BBB, JD Power, The Edison Award, Good Housekeeping Seal, Diabetic Foundation, etc.). Use press releases, social media, and/or good, old-fashioned "send them your product directly" tactics to target these third parties. Find out their criteria and earn the approval that you can. Using my failure again, I now know that I need to diversify to receive Best Seller recognition from other notable sources, like USA Today, Huffington Post, Inc. Magazine, and major metropolitan newspapers. I will be getting this book in front of the right reviewers and resellers in order to make this happen. How are you making sure your product and message gets in front of the right person in the right way?

3. PRICING SWAYS CONSUMER WILLINGNESS TO TRY A PRODUCT – EVEN IF THEY ARE SKEPTICAL

For release week, I ran a special on the e-version of my book – you could download it for only $0.99. I was allowing people to download advice that took me 15 years and more than $20 million dollars to acquire for less than a dollar. Why? Because book readers don't know me, and whether they loved the title, thought it was indecent, or were not even in the market for female entrepreneurial advice, the price was too good to pass up. Now, I exposed 6,000 people to my brand in just one week. This means 6,000 more people now know that I can take their consumer product national using TV, Radio, and Online faster, more efficiently, and for less than they thought possible. At my company, Synergixx, one of my clients is potentially worth $2-4M in gross annual billings. Imagine if only 2% of the people who purchased this book visited www.synergixx.com, and of that 2%, only 1% did business with me. That's another $2-4M in gross annual billings to my bottom line. If I were a Best Seller, maybe I could charge more for my speaking engagements – but not millions more. So, is selling more books more important than making the Best Seller lists? Or does making the list help to sell more books? Think about it! If the books that made the Best Seller list when mine was "passed over" had priced their new book similarly to mine in that week, perhaps they would have been #1 or #2 and I would have legitimately NOT made the list. Price matters when attracting new customers into your pipeline for long term customer revenue. Should you sell your product/service for $0.99 as an introductory price? Probably not! There is a magic formula – I specialize in it – and you need to consider it before your next marketing campaign.

4. FIGURE OUT HOW YOUR COMPETITION IS DOING IT – THEN DO IT BETTER

When I take on a new client, I spend weeks learning about their competition and the best practices in their category. As an author, I totally missed the boat on this one. I don't mean that I should have searched out all the other women writing a book about how they failed their way to success over the course of 15 years. Nor should I have researched the women who used body parts in the title of their business book to bring home an important message. I'm referring to how other UNKNOWN authors, like me, are making these lists. As I sat around on the Thursday after the Best Seller list was released, I started Googling and wondering what it would have been like to be a Wall Street Journal Best Seller. Then I came across a blog by Tim Grahl. This blog would have been RIDICULOUSLY HELPFUL before I embarked on my marketing campaign to make the Best Seller list! I literally smacked myself in the face after reading it.

I further researched book marketing techniques and discovered Michael R. Drew, owner of PromoteABook.com and his system for getting books to the top of these lists. He would have been worth a phone call before I went to press.

Whether you are trying to sell a book, launch a monthly membership program, sell supplements on autoship, or create a lead flow for your law practice, you need to understand how your competition is doing it. This allows you to recreate their success by improving upon their systems and excluding dead weight. I do this all day long for my clients but forgot about it when it came to my own product. I was too close to it, as you probably are to your product. If you are not as successful as you want to be, it is because you have failed at pinpointing why others like you are successful, both in business and in life.

5. START EARLIER AND REPEAT – PEOPLE NEED TO BE REMINDED TO ACT NOW!

When a client comes to me and says "I want to launch a TV infomercial with a celebrity in the next forty-five days to support my retail sales," I say, "We should have started 6 months ago!" Can I negotiate a celebrity contract, write a script, produce an infomercial, and get it on national TV in forty-five days? YES, and I do it very successfully! Does it always have the direct impact on retail sales that my clients need in that short period of time? Not always. Frequency builds desire and audience awareness. The concept of ACT NOW is dwindling because consumers know they can get products anytime, anywhere – so why bother ACTING NOW? If a product marketer wants to sell their new vegetable slicer in Walmart and use an infomercial to support store sales, they need to start airing that commercial six months or more prior to ever being on a store shelf. This allows consumers to start seeing the product repeatedly, so that when they see the new vegetable slicer on the shelf at Walmart six months later, their desire to BUY IT NOW is activated. The infomercial audience will pay the bills for direct sales until that day, and Walmart is more likely to carry your product if you are already established on TV. This same model is true whether you are using video on YouTube, Facebook, or Instagram to drive sales to Amazon, retail, or direct.

Don't wait to start advertising your product before your big sales push. I should have been marketing *Brains, Boobs, & Balls* in January through all channels so that when I decided to make a large marketing push in one week, my earlier efforts and the frequency of my message could carry the day. I still would have failed to be on the Best Seller list, but the takeaway is that you need to start marketing your product, service or new idea NOW, even if you are not completely ready.

So, regardless of which title is your pick, I now invite you to read about the 17 Lessons I learned while FAILING my way to success over the last 15 years building a business, family, and personal life. Please turn the page and look beneath my sheets…

BRAINS BOOBS & BALLS
CHARLIE FUSCO
CHARLIE FUSCO
BRAINS
BOOBS
& BALLS
LIFE LESSONS FROM THE ROAD ANY
FEMALE ENTREPRENEUR CAN USE.

Ladies, we that choose to be entrepreneurs will control the future of growth and prosperity in the world. Look at the facts.

According to the statistics from the Womenable report commissioned by American Express "OPEN State of Women-Owned Businesses 2015," the following is estimated:

- More than 9.4 million firms are owned by women, employing nearly 7.9 million people as of 2015.
- Women-owned firms account for 31% of all privately held firms and contribute 14% of employment and 12% of revenues.
- One in five firms with revenue of $1 million or more are woman-owned.

According to the National Women's Business Council (advisors to the President, Congress, and SBA)

- If women-owned firms were not in the economy and generating an estimated $2.8 trillion in economic impact, an additional 16 percent of our labor force would be jobless – that's 23 million people!

According to INC.com 2015

- Women entrepreneurs in the United States rank their happiness at nearly three times that of women who are not entrepreneurs or established business owners.

We are evolving into a legion of badass women of the future.

Happy, well-funded, confident, highly visible female entrepreneurs with broad networks will make the economy stronger than ever before! In the long term as a society, we need to develop young girls into women with self-confidence, desire to innovate, and passion for economic prosperity, as they are the safeguards of the health of the global community. Here is our biggest challenge: become wildly successful female entrepreneurs WITHOUT holding ourselves back in any other area of our life. Build the future of commerce INCLUSIVE of building family, community and personal passions. Forget about work-life-balance and sacrifice nothing for success. Can it be done?

I say YES!

Let's create a phenomenal community of female entrepreneurs who create the businesses of the future and accept nothing less than amazing in the present!

Join our private discussion group:
http:\\www.thatgirlcharlie.com/community

{DEDICATIONS}

<u>**To My 4 Best Decisions Ever**</u>

Tom Fusco – You chose me and I couldn't be the woman I am without you. Thank you for never falling out of love with me despite every reason I gave you. Here's to eternity together.

Jake Fusco – You sparked the flame that shaped this journey. Thank you for reminding me every day that it is all worth it.

Ava Fusco – You taught me gratitude at the deepest level. Thank you for being my mirror every day so I can see my reflection clearly.

Angelina Fusco – You forced me to be relentless in my expectations. Thank you for showing me that I can always be stronger than the day before.

Table of Contents

"Don't walk a mile in my high heels.
They're too expensive and my favorite pair.
Get your own pair and let's ride in the limo, together, instead."
—*Charlie Fusco*

Reader Warning!

Should you read this book?

Perhaps you picked up this book to see what type of woman describes her journey with such brash, maybe even anti-feminist, words. Maybe a copy was given to you by a colleague who said: "Can you believe as a professional she chose this title?" Or you're a man who just couldn't resist because two of your most favorite nouns are in the title. In any case, you are reading this page, so I've done something right so far…

My hope is that you're a woman (or care about a woman)… like me… who has spent a lifetime juggling intellect, passion, and drive while trying to conquer personal insecurities and feel in control of your life. You're a flawed combination of many female stereotypes who wants to create her dream life – no matter what!

It's important for you to understand why I've written this book with such a shocking title. You see, until receiving a note after giving a business talk, I never thought I'd let anyone look under my sheets. As you turn the following pages, that's exactly what you'll be doing.

I am *that girl* they call Charlie. My business card announces that I'm the CEO of an Advertising and Marketing agency, a creative guru, and marketing strategist. My bank statement proves I'm an all-the-time parent, serious about her kid's education, who orders take-out too much so I have more time to play. My text messages reveal that my lover of nearly 20 years can still make me hot. Incredible family. Impressive education. Skyrocketing career. Dynamic life. The paper trail makes me look great – but once you've looked beneath my sheets – you'll discover all the messy details that never made it to my resume!

"After hearing you talk about how you used to hold your breath during business meetings so your 'boobs' wouldn't pop forward and take over the conversation I started laughing 'till I cried. I cried because I realized I have been holding my breath too. I have been suffocating myself. Seeing you up there laughing at your pain and struggles made me see I can get through mine. I just wanted to say thank you for today." - Nahida

Nahida's note, left on my chair while I was in the restroom, stopped me in my tracks. I had screwed up my business talk and accidentally blurted out a comment about my boobs. Had this small admission about how insecure I was about my DD chest inspired another person? My 'boob' issues inspired this 65-year old lady? I wondered how many other women have lived for decades holding their breath too, for similar reasons. Was base humor what someone needed to stop holding their breath? It was on that day that I took *uncomfortable action. Truly uncomfortable.* I decided to share my journey publically and began to write this book. Then as I began to write, the voice in my head became loud and disruptive.

What am I thinking? I can't write this! I'm not ready for this! Share my real story? I'm not good enough yet. I don't have all the answers. And my past decade plus in business, in life, has been one mistake after another – that doesn't make me an expert on anything!

Then my husband said, "I bet people would be more interested in your screw-ups then your success. You've screwed up more than most people have tried. Stop apologizing."

He had a point. What was I apologizing for; who was I apologizing too? I failed. I survived. I succeeded. I am happy. Living on my terms. And still going strong. I've been blessed to build a company that has employed thousands of people in more than a decade marked by a deep recession, creating jobs when others were downsizing. I've created opportunities for my employees that far exceeded their expectations. My clients have sold millions of dollars of their products as a result of my work. I'm an established expert in my industry, a multimedia content generator, published author, motivational speaker, and I get to work with extraordinary people every day. After more than two decades of blood, sweat and tears, I've reached a level of expertise that now allows me to command top dollar for my time. Finally, after the long hours of building a business, raising three children more amazing than I can describe to you here, and growing my marriage into more than I could ever expect, I can now look at myself in the mirror and truthfully say 'I think I got this lingerie thing on lock down.' It wasn't by accident.

- A thirty-something woman with a steady career, lots of friends, her own apartment, and frequent flyer miles tells me that she has already given up on finding a soul mate because men find her difficult – HELL- TINDER WAS INVENTED FOR WOMEN LIKE HER, she says.
- An almost fifty-year-old woman with a half grown family, a mortgage, five weeks of vacation, and a dusty gym membership tells me that one day I'll understand husbands aren't all they're cracked up to be – THAT'S WHY GOD INVENTED NETFLIX, she asserts!
- A mother of two, who has spent more than a decade happily raising her family, her husband's career providing the income, discovers she likes to paint. She has supportive girlfriends and yet is unsatisfied, restless – BUT NO COMPLAINTS. SHE HAS A GOOD FAMILY, she pardons.
- A twenty-something college graduate with a better-than-average job, parental support, and a boyfriend who treats her well, complains her life is devoid of opportunities– COOL STUFF NEVER HAPPENS TO HER, she laments.
- A forty-something woman who built her business from scratch, loves her younger boyfriend, bought a $1000 pair of shoes because she can, and is learning to cook Thai, breaks down

crying because she missed out on having a family – AND NOW IT'S TOO LATE, she is positive!

These are all real women whom I have worked with over the years. I said the same thing to each one: **You have the brains to transform your world – you have amazing boobs - just have the balls to live life on your terms!**

- **Stop complaining**
- **Stop whining**
- **Stop making excuses**
- **Stop justifying**
- **Stop predicting**
- **Stop bracing for the fall**
- **Stop being afraid to say out loud what you deeply want.**
- **Stop trying to predict the future - live it!**
- **Get out of your own way!**

It's time you took *uncomfortable action*. I can say this to women with full authority because I had to stop all of the above too. For years, I've taken all the stuff that wouldn't look good on paper and hid it *beneath my sheets*, sometimes feeling so scared or embarrassed that hiding my head under the sheets was the only thing I could think to do. My messy journey as a work-in-progress mother, flawed wife, overly complicated woman, could-be-better friend, workaholic creator, and optimistic entrepreneur is what's beneath my sheets.

All women have a brain and boobs – both powerful assets. It's how we grow into confident risk-takers that make us successful entrepreneurs that can have it all simultaneously. This is why we must develop our own set of balls!

Forget about work/life balance – it's over rated! If I had tried to achieve work-life balance in the beginning of my career, I would have failed. Think about a balancing scale. To keep it even you have to remove things from one side until it balances with the other side. I am not willing to take things out of certain parts of my life just to feel balanced on the other side. I prefer successfully and happily unbalanced. This book is not a guide to finding a man/woman or running the perfect business or a road-map for being a good parent. It's about putting more play, passion, and progress into every area of your life. It's about living every aspect of your life with equal passion, commitment, and vigor. As you read through you'll notice three things:

- You'll disagree with some of it; you might even find it offensive.
- The narrative weaves in and out of three distinct areas of my life – business, family, personal – so you'll feel the twisty path of discovering what it takes to go from a girl to a chick to a lady both in business and in life.
- My perspective often changes from an entrepreneur to a scientist, woman, man, girlfriend, or a parent. When you want it all at the same time, you have to go in and out of these roles fluidly.

This book is an answer to a question I get asked often, *'How do you do it ALL at the same time?'*

Here's the honest, in-your-face, and non-PC answer.

> **It's fucking hard!**
> **So what! Stop whining!**
> **Make it happen!**
> **Anything less is just boring!**

Let my answer, set the tone for our conversation. These are my essential life lessons for creating a successful business, incredible family, and amazing sex life – simultaneously and without compromise. You may find my delivery brash, opinionated, direct, crude, and edgy, but also nakedly truthful. It will feel awkward and messy. I don't want you to be passive or comfortable as you receive the information. I want you finishing the book uncomfortable in your situation and inspired to take *uncomfortable action*. It's the key to becoming a fierce and fearless female entrepreneur.

Having it all at the same time takes **brains** (owning your intellect), **boobs** (creating your physical presence) and **balls** (confidently gambling on yourself).

My ultimate success has come from this ribald concept. I believe in my brains. I stopped apologizing for the boobs God gave me. And I grew a pair of balls – big ones. All that, and I kept my sense of humor along the way.

In these pages, you will find a very personal, comical, and raw account of my life and how I made a mess of it, lived through it, and am thriving as a result. I literally *failed-up* to success.

Knowing all of this, are you open to the TMI that is about to make us fast friends?

Just A Tease

The most effective way to do it, is to do it.
—*Amelia Earhart (1897-1939), American aviation pioneer*

Becoming an entrepreneur is like learning how to fly. You learn the steps, practice the execution, and put in the hours and the miles. But ultimately, you need the guts to navigate through the clouds when you can't see where you're going.

LET'S BEGIN AT AGE 11

My father loved to tell me that deciding to do something meant you had to do it – despite it all! The way he saw it, if you didn't stick by your decisions you'd train yourself NOT to make decisions and become a slave to the choices of others. I can clearly remember him saying this two dozen times or more before I left home.

The first time, I was eleven and nursing a bloody nose. His name was Daniel Harp. The place was the bridge near my school. Walking up behind me with his three friends, he started by flicking my neck just below my Paige-boy hairline. He was determined to get me to react, but I just kept walking. About five steps away from where the bridge turned into a sidewalk, frustrated with my lack of reaction, he lifted my T-shirt up over my head and then burst out laughing.

"She tapes her titties!"

All of the boys got a good look at my "early birds" wrapped tightly under three layers of duct tape. They were hysterical. I knew the sky was blue just like I knew I would lose this fight. But my gut told me I had to punch him in the face if I had any chance of living down the duct tape discovery. I took the first swing, and the next two, hitting him squarely in the face each time before the other three boys pinned me against the side of the bridge. Daniel got his swings in – my nose and "early birds" taking a good beating. When it was over, we both walked away to opposite sides of the bridge. I wasn't crying even though I wanted to. Daniel wasn't talking. The three boys seemed shocked that Daniel and I just walked away.

On my mile-long walk home, I ignored anyone that asked if I was okay or even glanced in my direction. I was not okay. My chest was aching, my nose was bleeding, and I was humiliated! I was the only girl in fifth grade that had to worry about wearing a bra, and now everyone would know that I used duct-tape to hide my growing chest. I was already the weird kid; now I was something much worse. My father cleaned up my face. He was unclear as to the real reason I had thrown the first punch. I didn't want him to find out about the duct tape too. He told me the swelling would go down before school in the morning. I begged him not to force me to go to school. How could he want me to be on the same playground where Daniel and the other boys would be laughing it up? I begged. I pleaded. I produced tears. He wouldn't budge even as he wiped the blood from my face. He said it was my decision to throw the first punch.

"Make your decision and live through it. If it doesn't work out, then make the decision *right* the next time. There's always a next time, Charlie – if you're the one making the decisions. Tomorrow, just show up smiling!"

My life was over, and he wanted me to *show up smiling*? To my total surprise, Daniel was not at school the next day or the next. No one knew about the duct tape or at least didn't mention it. Instead, rumor had it that Daniel's father gave him quite a beating for fighting with a girl and coming home with his own bloody nose.

Later that same day, the principal called me into his office and asked me if anything had happened with Daniel. I said no. He pressed me, and I kept saying no. The small victory on the bridge was now mine. I determined that Daniel would leave me alone because I said so, not because the principal made him.

The rest of the school year, no matter how many times we ran into each other in class, in the cafeteria, or on the playground, Daniel and I never spoke about the incident. And to my surprise, I didn't hate him. In a strange way, I respected him. He never talked about the incident. He never tried to belittle me for it or change the facts. He let it be what it was: two kids being hot headed and using poor judgment on a bridge. But just in case, I stopped taping down my "early birds" for the rest of the school year.

I was the weird, smart girl who dressed like a boy, had a bowl-cut hairdo, played catcher on an all-boys all-star baseball team, filled out a bra like a champ, and still wanted the girls to invite me to their Cabbage Patch Kid parties. My decision on that bridge was NOT to let anyone push me around because of these things. If I had stayed home the next day, I would have left my confidence on that bridge. Staying home would have apologized for my decision. Right or wrong, my silence in the principal's office was ME taking responsibility for throwing the first punch.

I didn't know it then, yet it is clear to me today. By forcing me to go to school the next day, my father made me stand up for my decision – to feel the effects of it, to live through it, so I could understand its power, and more importantly know that I would be able to handle whatever came next. The idea began to form in my head that I could take care of myself… I was beginning to grow a pair.

<u>Skip to Age 24</u>

I was only 24 when I became a CEO and New Mother. I didn't read the instruction manual to either.

One morning, preparing for a pitch with a company that would ultimately become my catalyst client, I focused on three things: the

$8.07 in my business account, breast pads and safety pins. I was dressing for a boardroom meeting with an all-male company that had just received first round funding from an Angel Investor. I was nervous. There was not enough duct tape in the world to hide my new mother 44FF chest! Yes, it's okay to take a moment to process that visual!

My 44FF's had a mind of their own; swelling, leaking, burning, and pulsating at their will. It was as if lactation aliens had colonized my chest. Not only were my "early birds" now the size of large cabbage heads, they had decided to squirt out milk unexpectedly and frequently – without my permission.

I was wearing a charcoal suit because at age 24, I still believed a suit would make me equal to a man in the boardroom – that hiding behind clothing would make my brain the center of attention. My suit was busting at the seams. Four safety pins held the button down blouse together; another three safety pins held the jacket closed at my waist, while four breast pads struggled to hold in a tidal wave of breast milk. I looked in the mirror. *"You've got this!"* But! When you can't control your body, confidence is an illusion.

I walked into the boardroom and was the only woman. It didn't faze me. That was normal for me. At my last company, I started my career in 'boys only boardrooms.' I was able to hang in the bars and strip clubs with the boys to earn their attention in business matters. Not to mention, I was overly prepared for the pitch and over qualified for the project. There was no reason I could think of that I wouldn't get this job that I badly needed to stay in business. I was still very nervous, but I showed up to the boardroom smiling.

As I went through the Power Point presentation, I could feel the safety pins under my shirt straining, and the building wetness behind the breast pads. The chairs in the boardroom were low to the ground and as I sat at the table my 44FF's sat atop the table. When the men were talking, I held my breath. I didn't want my boobs to take over the conversation. I didn't want my breathing to create motion in my chest area that would take attention away from the meeting. If I held my breath, they wouldn't notice my boobs propped on the table like bowling balls.

And if I didn't breathe too much the safety pins would hold, and the milk would not flow. I held my breath so my breasts would not pop forward and become the center of attention.

When it was my turn to speak, I did so loudly and quickly so they would look at my mouth and focus on my words. It didn't matter. Every time I opened my mouth six sets of eyes would wander away from my face towards my 44FFs. It was like I was back on that bridge with six Daniel Harps laughing at me behind their professional demeanors. Duct tape. Breast pads. It was all about what was under my shirt.

I moved through the presentation alternating between holding my breath and talking quicker than I should. When it was clear that the "gentlemen" were making under-their-breath comments about my 'huge titties' I forced myself not to turn red by creating a movie in my head.

My 44FFs started shooting milk at the men who I wanted as clients - machine gun style. Tat- Tat-Tat-Tat-Tat! Tit that you SOBs! The six of them were quickly covered in white liquid and writhing on the boardroom floor. But I digress...

I knew I was struggling to keep their attention on what I could offer them in business. My body was betraying me. I was red under the collar, sweating from the stress and the need to feed a baby they didn't know I had. I kept my baby a secret in business. To them, I wasn't a new Mom. I was a young girl with a large chest playing the role of business woman. I was losing this business for reasons out of my control. I was still that awkward girl on the bridge but this time, I didn't know how to throw the first punch.

"Great presentation Charlie. Your reputation precedes you. But we're just not convinced that a shop your size can handle such a large project."

I forced tears back, swallowing their salty taste. The truth was, I wasn't convinced I could handle it either.

What made me think I could pull off my company? My reputation belongs to my previous employer. They aren't buying the solo Charlie. I am too young. The reality is that I can't get taken seriously on my own. What am I thinking?

They started to collect their things. These gentlemen didn't deserve my reputation or attention. Thinking about the $8.07 in my bank account, I allowed my bruised ego and the negative chatter in my mind to take over.

As they began to stand up, I let out a sharp breath and then I felt it. There was a wet spot that had broken through the charcoal suit on my left side. A tiny, but spreading, wet dot emphasizing that I couldn't handle something of any real size. I flipped my hair around to try and cover the wetness. It was too short because I had just cut it thinking that business women should have shoulder length hair to be competitive with the boys. I turned my shoulders inward to hide it. I shifted lower in my chair to get the spot out of their eye line which only made the table edge cut my breasts in half and cause more leaking. I stood up pulling my notepad close to my chest.

"I understand gentlemen. So let me prove it to you. I'll do the project for half the cost. When it works, you'll give me your next project a full rate."

I said this with a huge smile on my face to their astonishment. I got into the car only minutes later and hurriedly hooked up the breast pump while putting the car in drive. As the humming sound started, I was sure that small pieces of my soul were being sucked up with my milk. I made a mental note to throw the milk away so that my six-month old son wouldn't drink any of my Loser Germs. I drove home pumping the whole way, refusing to look at the passenger in the car next to me, watching me pump with one hand and steer with the other. As the humming of the breast pump became white noise, I tried not to think about the check for a 50% deposit of the 50% discount I had burning a hole in my purse. I still believed my boobs were my problem...

FAST FORWARD TO AGE 35

"It's a million dollars a year, Charlie. Guaranteed. We'll move you out here. A new house as a bonus. Top schools for your kids. You call the shots. It's perfect for you. We need you. You can't say no. With my backing and your brains the sky's the limit."

A decade after starting my company, someone was willing to pay me a million dollars a year for my brains. I would not have believed it, but there it was on paper looking back at me in black ink with a dotted line. I was sitting at an Italian restaurant in Los Angeles being wined and dined. The offer was simple. Give up my company, run his, and sky-rocket my income. All this company wanted was my brains in exchange. The offer was in writing and demanded immediate acceptance.

"Are you okay, Charlie?"

"Yes, there is just so much garlic in my pasta my eyes are irritated." Bullshit! I was holding back tears and blaming the garlic. A million dollars! Moving expenses! A new house! Private schools! Run his company! No stress of running my company! I had arrived! I was finally good enough! I could stop holding my breath!

And then I felt this wave of guilt wash over me for wanting this opportunity so badly to happen. I wanted to accept the offer on the spot without checking with my family or my company. I was tired of being the business owner. Exhausted by the struggle, being an entrepreneur sucked. I could taste the guilty bitterness.

I asked for a day to discuss with my husband. He smiled because he thought I was acting coy.

"For me to take this job, you would have to leave the University. The kids would be set. We'd be set. But it has to be a joint decision." I stated the facts only.

My husband, the same man who sacrificed unconditionally while I built my business, looked me directly in the eye and said, "It's a great offer. I don't want to stop teaching, but it exceeds what we've been able to give our family. But we can also be happy the way things are now. I'll go to Los Angeles if you think the job is the right thing to do. I believe in you either way." He was stating facts too.

I declined the offer knowing the client would take his seven million dollars of business away from my company as a result. Losing the business was a kick in the stomach because of how hard I had worked to build it and how big a piece of revenue it represented on my P&L. It was the guilty feeling that helped me make the decision this time. If I had truly 'arrived,' I should not be feeling guilty. My guilt came from the fact that I was considering taking the easy road and going against my core drivers.

I knew I couldn't give up control of my life to build up someone else's company and ever feel good about it. I also knew that turning this down would cripple me financially in many ways. Unlike the last ten years of decisions, I was 100% okay with saying NO. Finally, I was confident my brains would get me through this, the negative outcome this decision would have on my business and beyond.

REFLECTING BACK...

I started my company only 13 years after walking home from that bridge, the same way I started that fight with Daniel. I decided to follow my gut instinct and threw the first punch; I took *uncomfortable action.* At the same time, I decided to start a family. I jumped into all these decisions with no less than 200% equal commitment. Deciding to do this all at the same time was easy – I was young and full of energy and dreams.

But!

Having to decide to keep doing it became near impossible. Recommitting to my decisions during some of the most challenging times in my life almost didn't happen. I had to get up every morning, look in the mirror and say, "Somehow, I CAN do this" – even when I didn't always believe it.

Many times, I let my circumstances cloud my vision. Allowed doubt to fill my head. I stopped deciding for myself. My I CAN'Ts became louder than my HOW CAN I's. In business, this means the difference between staying open and starting over. Personally, it destroys relationships and leads to the loneliest place you can ever imagine. Trust me; I've been there.

If you've chosen to read this book, it's because your passion is calling. That passion is bubbling inside your belly, or you may be so tired from your current path that you barely feel passionate about anything anymore. The passion is still there.

READY TO BECOME A FIERCE & FEARLESS ENTREPRENEUR?

The year I started my company I wanted it all. The future was bright, and it was my time. I had passion. I had ambition. I had talent. I had a supportive husband. What could go wrong?

What didn't go wrong?

I grew my business to more than seventeen million dollars in revenue in under ten years, then almost lost it all. I nearly bankrupted my company and my marriage. I lost both my parents, miscarried a child, developed a disease, fought through a recession, was betrayed in business by those I considered friends, and became the mother I swore I wouldn't. I allowed myself to be taken advantage of in business. My friendships became toxic. I got fat! I lost interest in sex! I lost connection with myself. How's that for being a successful female entrepreneur?

Mine is a story of fighting back without compromising. About turning my SCREW-UPS into FAIL-UPS. Becoming a woman that I admire. Finally, I decided that a positive P/L in the business world is as important as achieving multiple orgasms in my personal life. One cannot sacrifice for the other.

Part One

Defining Brains, Boobs, & Balls

===

I do not wish women to have power over men; but over themselves.
—*Mary Wollstonecraft*

===

Chapter One

Defining Brains, Boobs, & Balls

The three most important lessons in this book.

I am not an overall feminist. You may have figured that out from the title of the book. I do believe all **people** deserve equal rights in political, economic, and social standings despite their sex. I just don't subscribe to the fact that women should desire equality in the opportunities presented to them currently. Why do you want to have equal rights in your business, your family, and your bedroom when you are in control of your future? Equal to who? I think the kind of woman who will benefit from this book knows that she deserves better than equal rights. The entrepreneurial woman of the future is ready to define, design, and deliver her own set of opportunities.

Meet Mary Wollstonecraft. This chick was a bad-ass English writer, philosopher, and advocate of women's rights from 1759–1797. I consider her an entrepreneur for sure. Maybe you have a problem with me calling her a chick. I don't think Mary would give a damn, though. Why? I'm quoting her in a book over 200 years later.

If she had accepted equal treatment during her life, what would that have done for her? We'll never know because instead this woman entrepreneur decided to be unrealistic in her desires without apologizing for her actions or her successes. She wrote novels, treatises, a travel narrative, a history of the French Revolution, a conduct book, and a children's book, at a time when the British literacy rate for women was less than 50% and less than 80% of men.

Why be equal to men who weren't even at 100% during this time? See my point?

She's best known for penning *A Vindication of the Rights of Woman* (1792), in which she argues that women are not naturally inferior to men, but rather only appear to be because they lack education. She suggests that both men and women be treated as rational beings, and she imagined a social order founded on reason. I agree 500%! Women have nothing standing in their way of education these days. Google and YouTube are the great educational equalizers.

Wollstonecraft remains inspirational to me because, even in her short life span, she made it count in every area. Her personal life received more attention than her prolific writings until late in the 20th century because her choices were "unconventional"! She had two affairs, one with a painter and another with a diplomat. Imagine being a woman in those days, dreaming of equality, hearing gossip about this Mary chick who was writing books and boldly initiating relationships with anyone she chose. She was a secret inspiration to many women who, at that time, were fighting to become 'just equal.' Mary was not interested in equal, ordinary opportunities; she created extraordinary events. Of this, I am convinced.

Wollstonecraft didn't stop there. She went on to marry the philosopher William Godwin, one of the forefathers of the anarchist movement. How is that for personal branding as woman who didn't follow the rules? Mary died at 38, the same age I was when I started writing this book, and she went out with a bang by giving birth to Mary Wollstonecraft Godwin eleven days before her death. Her daughter grew up to become Mary Shelley – you know another bad ass chick - who wrote one of the greatest stories of all time, *Frankenstein*. Who wants to be equal when Frankenstein is waiting to be born?

Today, Wollstonecraft is regarded as one of the founding feminist philosophers, often cited for both her life and work as an important influencer. I believe, if she were alive today, she would publish a retraction on her feminist views; re-framing our mindset to focus NOT on equality for women but on women understanding they control the definitions and opportunities in their life.

A woman's bold actions take her further than accepting her current 'equal reality' ever will.

With this thought, let me further set the parameters for the rest of our conversation.

Lesson One: BRAINS (Owning Our Intelligence)

Female entrepreneurs are born with more than enough intelligence to find a solution to any problem.

Here's the thing ladies. Deciding to read this book means you're in the middle of, OR are about to, step foot on this entrepreneurial road traveled by few that is exciting and terrifying at the same time. Know that you're going to encounter one problem after another - and it is okay. You can handle it.

Ask yourself, at what age did you realize you were intelligent, passionate, and driven? I've known from a very young age that I can figure things out faster than others, create multiple solutions to a problem easier, and trust my intuition earlier than the majority of others my age or even older.

My first entrepreneurial experience was in the 5th grade. I was in charge of the Cookie Cart during lunch-time in the school cafeteria. My job was to sell cookies to students for $0.25 and put the money in the lock box. One day it occurred to me that I could spray Mint Binaca Blast (breath freshener) on the cookies and sell them as Mint Chocolate Chip cookies for $0.50. The lock box would get $0.25 and I would keep the other $0.25 since I had provided the Binaca Blast. My business worked; until three weeks later when I was called to the principal's office and was shut down – but not before I had made $24.50. I blame it on my genes.

I believe all entrepreneurial women have a 'gene' that drives them to think differently and desire the road less chosen. It is your genetic disposition that called you to read this book.

The female brain is made up of three areas: intelligence (brains), knowledge (facts, data, information), and intuition (gut feel). Combining them, you ignite passion, develop fierce abilities, make fearless decisions, and become hungry for more.

Our intellect allows us to soak up formal education, acquire data, and convert experiences into lessons like a super computer. Our intelligence is the speed at which our brains make sense of all this data and string it together into actions. We use it, along with our emotional IQ and keen intuition, to keep our pack (family, staff, and friends) safe, healthy and happy. Our growth and success are tied largely to the amount of facts, data, and information we acquire.

Successful female entrepreneurs are life-long learners that seek data every day in a wide variety of subjects. This consistent collection of data turns us into great leaders, inventors, and problem solvers.

In the past, education wasn't always accessible to women. Now there is no excuse for a lack of facts, data, or informed decisions. Our knowledge, or smarts, is now acquired at a rate that we determine. Now, more than ever, it easier to become a smarter woman… faster. There are no limits on acquiring the 'smarts' we need to super-succeed.

Being able to think faster, absorb information quicker, and have greater informed intuition, even when we are not the expert in a situation, gives us super powers.

Here is the real zinger – highly intelligent women are prone to confidence issues. Yes. We. Are.

Why

Once we are on the entrepreneurial road, we lose confidence in our intellectual abilities, which can lead us to give up sooner on ideas, dilute business, settle in relationships, shy away from our physicality and keep us from going after what we want immediately. We begin to see our success as 'luck rather than achievement'. A lack of intellectual confidence makes us dependent, careful, and apologetic.

WHY DOES IT HAPPEN TO THE BEST OF US?

First, higher intelligence can make us feel unaccepted in social groups, so we hide it, dim it, or worse we second guess it. In tense situations, we tend to succumb to emotional responses without collecting enough data, so our actions begin to feel risky and we question how 'smart we are.' Also, we may lean too heavily on 'smarts' ignoring our intuition because we don't want to risk the better outcome. All these reasons, separately or together, cause a lack of intellectual confidence. Where does it all start?

Growing up, my brains got me called out of class for IQ testing, put into the honor courses, nominated for regional and state scholarships, held to different standards by my teachers – none of which made me popular with my peers. They saw me as different and I hated it! So early on, being able to figure things out quickly was not a confidence booster.

Between the ages of 14-18, I never found a boy who wanted to date me because of my grades. All the honor classes, advanced placement, debate team, scholarships, and awards did not get me asked to Prom. Using my body language and flirting, on the other hand, worked so much better. I was a strict Tom Boy until 9th grade, so I had never wanted to feel like a pretty girl; in high school, it's all I wanted. When I started getting asked out on dates as a result of playing down my brains and playing up my boobs, it reinforced for me, true or not, that boys don't appreciate a girl's brains. I remember thinking that I would rather be a C student who was pretty than an A student who wasn't. Isn't that a crazy but also familiar thought?

When it came to the workplace, I experienced something similar. I needed to get a job quickly when I was thirteen because my parents were suddenly broke, so I lied about my age (at 5'10 and a C cup nobody questioned me.) I knew I was smart enough to get hired and get promoted fast. That was my goal. I was offered two jobs on the same day, and since I was desperate, I accepted them both – Kinko's Copy Shop after school and the balloon store on the weekends. My intelligence kicked in and allowed me to learn the businesses quickly. Sure enough, within two months at both jobs, I was promoted and given a raise. Except, I left work each day feeling terrible because my coworkers wanted nothing to do with me. They either saw me as a threat or worse, someone who would bring attention to how little effort they put in. I had the paycheck, but I felt like an outcast.

Explaining away your success as 'being given a chance and being lucky' is praised. Yet, accomplishment through applied intelligence can be socially unacceptable. It's a double edge-sword.

This disconnected relationship with my intelligence (my brains) was so dysfunctional that it began to reprogram how I thought of myself, how I acted in the world, and how I made decisions. For example, the year my business hit seventeen million dollars in gross revenue instead of thinking *'Wow – you did this! Keep going!'*

What I thought was, *'Wow! I'm so lucky. I'd better get smarter people in here who know how to run a business of this size.'*

Just when I had broken through the glass ceiling, I didn't trust ME. And it cost me dearly.

The key to success is owning our intelligence, understanding how to use it, putting it into action, and not apologizing for it.

Tech entrepreneur Clara Shih, who founded the successful social media company Hearsay Social in 2010 and joined the board of Starbucks at the age of twenty-nine, is one of the few female CEOs in the still macho world of Silicon Valley. Shih would go on to graduate with the highest GPA of any computer-science major in her class, and was quoted as saying sometimes she "felt like an imposter." Facebook COO Sheryl Sandberg was quoted a year before her book *"Lean In"* was published, "There are still days I wake up feeling like a fraud, not sure I should be where I am."

Why didn't these highly successful women just say, 'I'm a smart, intelligent woman who gathered the facts, followed my gut, and worked harder than the other person for my well-earned achievement?'

In my time working with thousands of women and hundreds of moms in business, I've observed that the more success we women achieve, the more and more we tend to doubt ourselves. We give credit where credit isn't due… other people. It's like the better we get, the less we believe it.

In my case, I assumed that book-smart, older-than-me businessmen could handle my company's growth better than I could. After all, what did I know about running a business?

How could I possibly learn fast enough to sustain a seventeen-million-dollar company? So, I hired an executive staff, **paid them more than I was making,** and essentially gave them control of my growing company.

That's when the problems started. The economy tanked. Competition became fierce. Employees were poached. Debt rapidly increased. One problem spawned another. It was less than two years later, and my company had slipped fast towards bankruptcy with millions of dollars of debt and a massive reduction in revenue. All the executives I had hired couldn't run my company during these trying times. I underestimated that in business, like in life, reaction speed and intuition are equal, maybe more important, to knowledge. The problems my business was experiencing needed intelligent thinking and fearless intuition to go along with informed decision-making. It also needed someone to take full responsibility for the outcome.

As I surveyed the scene of my crumbling business, I was stressed 24/7. So stressed that I gained 55 pounds and my scalp was always peeling. I couldn't sleep for more than 3 hours at a time. I got through the day with coffee and delusion. I was afraid all the time. I felt dumb, stupid, little, inadequate, and helpless. I didn't want anyone to know the truth, so I faked that everything was under control. It was exhausting. After everything I had survived for thirty plus years, I felt like I couldn't fix it. How could someone as intelligent as I let this happen? Simple.

I was relying on other people's pedigree. More importantly, I wasn't using my intellectual advantage to rapidly assimilate data, connect the dots, and execute the quickest solutions. My higher intelligence meant I could have asked more questions, taken classes, gone to seminars, read books, hired a consultant, or gotten some education from other business owners and then used what I learned to run my business. If my lack of confidence as a business woman made me scared and vulnerable in the office, imagine the kind of mother and wife it made me!

My intelligence has served as one of my greatest strengths, my ass-saving fallback, a spark for my creativity, and my safety blanket!

Other times I've squandered its currency making it my greatest weakness and source of shame. There were times I played down my intelligence or rented it out for the success of others.

Until one day, with my screw-ups piling up and threatening to bury me, I simply decided I would succeed despite my failures. I

decided to be 100% responsible for any outcome. I decided to bet it all on my intellect, smarts, and intuition.

Ladies, own your intelligence. Know that you are gifted with the ability to think quicker, grasp complexity easier, and have greater informed intuition. These are gifts. They mean nothing without learning and hard work but they are still gifts. These gifts are one reason you have the entrepreneurial fire in your belly. People are going to love, hate, ignore or be inspired by you, in part, because they can see how intelligent you are and who you are a result of it.

Female entrepreneurs need to commit to get smarter every day so when you need data it is ready and waiting:

- read books on multiple subjects
- take classes or online courses on topics outside your business
- join masterminds
- watch documentaries on your industry
- listen to podcasts in multiple categories
- hire a life or business coach
- attend seminars on wealth management and corporate vision
- engage in peer discussions on blogs or networking events
- host dinner parties and invite people you want to learn from
- volunteer your time in organizations

The opportunities to educate yourself are endless. The funny thing is, admitting you are seeking knowledge, and trying to learn to be better, is a challenge for many women. It's like we don't want people to see us without our super-hero cape on. Give it up. Openly seek data and education daily.

Every day is a school day, ladies. By making data acquisition part of your daily routine you build both your intellectual confidence and your 'smarts' amplifying your informed intuition.

Now when you face a stressful situation, or you come up against a problem, or you need to make tough decisions quickly, all three areas of your brain are maximized, and you feel more in control. You become **fiercely** independent, **fearless**, and unapologetic.

BRAIN BUILDING RESOURCES

SIZE MATTERS, ladies. The bigger your network, the bigger your access to data, facts and experiences that fuel your intelligence and intuition. Research shows entrepreneurs with larger networks grow bigger business. Besides Google, Facebook, YouTube and LinkedIn (some of the greatest educational resources for women in business) I submit a list of business-specific resources to grow your network and access.

- **Acceleration:** Upstart Accelerator, and Women's Startup Lab
- **Certification:** Women's Business Enterprise National Council (WBENC)
- **Leadership training on accessing equity finance:** Astia and digitalundivided
- **Networking:** Ellevate, Girls Raising, National Association of Women's Business Owners and SheEO
- **Peer advisory groups/CEO Masterminds):** Women Presidents' Organization, Maverick1000, and E-Women's Network
- **Training for angel investing:** 37 Angels and Pipeline Fellowship
- **Women-led venture capital funds:** 1315 Capital, Aligned Partners Capital Efficient Companies, Aspect Ventures, Astarte Ventures, Astia Angels, BELLE Capital, Broadway Angels, Canaan Partners, Cowboy Ventures, Double Bottom Line Venture Capital, Illuminate Ventures, Kapor Capital, Launch Angels, Springboard Fund, Starvest Partners, Women's Capital Connection and Women's Venture Capital Fund

Lesson Two: BOOBS
(Creating Your Dynamic Physical Presence)

Female entrepreneurs must always put a high value on creating a dynamic and powerful physical presence.

As an entrepreneur, your job is to birth new ideas and sell them into reality by keeping people passionate about exploiting the success of your ideas. Your body confidence, your personal style, how you carry yourself, and your physical reactions during situations all impact how you inspire people.

I'm a firm believer that our bodies change our brains, our brains can change our actions, and our actions change our outcomes. When we learn how to exist in our body positively, imperfections and all, we can energize any room and create empowered action. **We have a physical energy that is both confident and sexual in nature; it exudes through our body language.** It's in how we carry ourselves and even how we hold a standing or sitting position.

What does it exactly mean to create a dynamic and powerful physical presence?

We've all met a woman who is a "hot mess" in the looks department. She lacks physical grace, even snorts when she laughs, and yet she is getting all the attention. If you're over 30, then you know that whether you are trying to power network, meet the love of your life, or just look hot in the bedroom, commanding a room has nothing to do with perfect features and designer clothes. So, what does the 'hot mess' have that you don't?

It's inevitable that we will have to talk about my boobs so let's get to it. In 5th grade, they popped out overnight to a B+ cup, and I tried to hide them. By 9th grade, I was a C+ cup but had no clue what to do with them – by 11th grade I figured it out. When I gave birth to my

13

son Jacob, I was a 44FF which I'm positive qualified me for the circus. I've now settled into a very comfortable… drum roll please… 38 DD. When I first got into business I wore gray and brown pantsuits because I thought they hid my breasts and made people take me more seriously. When I would get home and take off the suit jacket, I would look in the mirror and see all the buttons on the blouse straining. I saw a very manly person staring back at me. It made me feel unattractive. I looked at myself and felt like I was wearing my father's clothes – worse – that to be taken serious I had to dress this way. When I would wear tight fitting shirts, which is not hard at my size, I felt ogled.

I was either the 'she-man in a suit' or the 'slutty secretary'. It was my fault, not theirs, because I didn't know how to hold my body in either the business suit or the tight shirt. I didn't know how to be visually appealing and command respect at the same time. I didn't own my boobs. Sounds crass but it is true.

For me it was boobs. For you, it might be a short stature, your weight, your nose, the fact that you're too pretty, a big forehead, a scar, stretch marks, or any number of other "flaws" women have admitted that bother them.

We grow up being told not to judge a book by its cover – it's the inside that counts. Physical looks don't matter. Blah, blah, blah. We don't like to admit it but how people react to us, and how we look at ourselves, physically impacts how we move through the world. **Ignoring the impact of our physical body is as bad as, maybe worse than, doubting our intelligence.**

I had to change my thinking: 'business appropriate' doesn't matter any longer, instead I wear what I feel is a respectful and authentic representation of myself. I stopped wearing brown and gray business suits that made me look like clip art for 'corporate women'. I took off the corporate costume and started wearing clothes that made me feel like me: business attire with a sexy edge. Something as simple as wearing a dress to a business meeting is so liberating. Why? I had pigeon-holed myself into thinking that to play in the boy's boardroom I had to dress like a boy to be taken seriously. When I finally said 'suits make me look heavy, frumpy and my boobs bigger than normal' and changed my perspective to 'this dress fits my curves, the right bra makes my boobs look great, and I feel comfortable in this fabric' it changed everything:

- How I smiled when I shook hands with people
- How I sat in chairs
- How I walked down the hallway
- How I held my shoulders when leaning forward to make a point
- How I was able to call on my feminine voice in heated meetings to diffuse situations
- How I was able to shock and awe when the 'pretty girl' in the dress had brains, too

I decided that hiding my physical sexuality was a waste of time and delayed progress. I made the mental shift that it was perfectly acceptable to be smart and sexy at the same time. It was my birth right. My wardrobe went from clip art business suits to bold expressions of every facet of my personality. Do I always wear dresses? No way. I've worn leather pants and motor cycle boots to meetings. I decide on what I am trying to get out of any situation – business or personal – and then I dress in a way that makes me feel confident and sexy for that situation. Yes, smart, confident and sexy. Why would I dress any other way? What better combination is there in preparing to win?

Remember, sexy is a feeling not the amount of skin you are showing. **Sexy is a woman who knows her mind, respects her body, and enjoys that everyone around her knows it.**

Female entrepreneurs are like a very rare and valuable book with information that is in high demand. Our outside cover must reflect this rarity for the largest amount of people to open up to us and see what we have to offer in the world. Creating our dynamic physical presence goes far beyond cleavage, ladies. It is an intentional act designed to create intentional reactions.

Until we are 200% inspired by how we look in our body and can command attention with our physical presence we cannot be fully successful or completely happy.

When we embrace the physical assets that make us happy, make peace with the parts that don't, and enhance the rest as needed, we become powerful and joyful.

I've been pregnant four times, battled a disease that kept me 55 lbs heavier than I should be, and had emergency surgery that left my body scared. Even the belly button God gave me lives in a different zip code on my stomach than when I was born. I have seen my body morph over the years in shocking ways. There was a time I would only lay in bed facing away from my husband because I was so uncomfortable in my skin and didn't trust what I looked like asleep – so better keep my body out of his sight line.

It was my responsibility to get to a place that when I stood in the bathroom mirror, I saw the sexual power in my reflection. Yes, sexual power. You can't look in the mirror and say "that doesn't look too bad." You have to look in the mirror and say "that's worthy of a shag today!" I spent years apologizing to myself for how my body incited "inappropriate" reactions. Then I spent years looking at my post-baby body wondering if I could still create an inappropriate reaction at all.

Once I was able to embrace my assets, pay reverence to my imperfections, and realize the rest looks great with a little smoke and mirrors, controlling other people's reactions became easier. More importantly, my words became more powerful coming out of my mouth with a confident physical presence.

Whatever makes you feel awkward in your skin is also what makes you stand out in the world. Stand tall, show case it, dress it up, bring attention to it. Embrace your assets.

- Look at Owen Wilson. He has broken his nose so many times that it became crooked. Rather than have it fixed, like many in Hollywood would do, he decided to embrace it as an asset. He and his crooked nose reek of sex appeal on screen. We celebrate his assets.

- Mick Jagger looked in the mirror and realized that his huge lips were not going anywhere, and they became his iconic trademark because he presented them unapologetically.
- Dolly Parton created her own assets surgically with much criticism and yet has inspired millions with her talent and generosity.
- Oprah Winfrey won over the world with her smile despite her lifelong weight struggle and unconventional looks.

RESEARCH TO CONSIDER

- Malcolm Gladwell's best-selling book "Blink" states that, accurate or not, we form judgments very quickly based on facial expressions and body language.
- Amy Cuddy, a social psychologist at Harvard Business School, talks about the rewards of holding a Power Pose. She contends that when you stand in your Power Pose for 2 minutes at any given time, your testosterone (dominant, powerful, strong) hormonal levels go up by 20% and your cortisol (stress, fear, anxiety) hormonal levels drop by 25%. It's significant – even if you think her % is high – any increase at all in feeling strong and powerful and any decrease in stress and anxiety is worth it.
- Princeton University Psychologist, Alex Todorov, has shown that it takes a tenth of a second for someone to form an opinion of us.

As an entrepreneur, how you come across in that crucial tenth of a second can dictate if they buy into your vision or not. As a mother, how people react to you in front of your kids is key to giving them confidence in themselves. And as a woman trying to attract another human being it can mean the difference between explosive sex and Chinese take-out for one! Ask yourself, in every situation, are you putting forth your most powerful physical self?

CREATING A DYNAMIC AND POWERFUL PHYSICAL PRESENCE

Ladies, step one is the superficial stuff. Is your 'book cover' as appealing as it can be to the world? Spend time considering your wardrobe. Does it reflect your spirit? Spend some money on a stylist to learn what flatters you. Get make-up lessons. Take time to develop your personal style. Get your hair blown out professionally once a week – it does wonders for your productivity. It's true – when your hair looks great, you feel great! Will all this superficial stuff make you more successful in business and relationships? Yes. And no. There is more to it.

When I tell women to 'use your boobs' I am referring to how we hold and present our physical energy when we walk into a room. When you downplay your assets, your physical energy is negative and weaker – forgettable. When you embrace them, your physical energy is positive and contagious; most importantly memorable.

Aside from my fashion addiction, make-up routine, and shoe collection here are specific things I do that create my dynamic, powerful, physical presence.

STAND TALLER

If I'm honest, I grew up with a complex around my height, my man shoulders and my "porn-star tits". I never felt physically graceful, beautiful, or powerful. Whenever possible I did not stand up tall. I lowered my shoulders. I wore clothes that covered up my breasts. I sat lower in chairs. The result was that I ended up surrounded by people who would take advantage of this – in a meeting or on a date because my body language didn't match my spoken words.

How often have you found yourself slouching, collapsing from your midsection and reducing your height? Psychologically, on some level, we've all done it, and the result is that our spoken words have less impact and less power.

Confident, empowered people own their height and are not afraid of being seen. At 5'10 I'm naturally tall. I still make it a habit of walking into any room standing like I am 6'1. Yes, I often wear heels that make me this tall but that's not the trick. I intentionally exaggerate my height.

My shoulders are back. My back is arched. My breasts are forward. My chin is up. I stand taller. Even if you are five feet tall this works. Whenever possible, I stand in between the person and the door. When near steps, on one step higher. Or choose the bar stool over the regular table. I position my body above others. I will even stand on tip toe occasionally at the exact moment I want to make a point. Why? What I find is that my posture changes how people react to me. When I am standing taller, it changes my physical energy. Plus, lingerie looks better when you stand up tall! I'm a big fan of seduction on tip toe!

TAKE UP MORE SPACE

Think of the last time you were at an important meeting or with a group – how much space did you take up? When I first got into the business, I would sit in a meeting with my hands underneath the table or glued to my side. When I was standing at a networking event, I'd cross my arms. Especially, when I was in groups with bigger, stronger personalities I would try to make myself smaller – try to fit in. And it wasn't just business. It was the same at parties, in bars, at night clubs. Regardless of where I was, I was trying to take up less space. Even in bed, I would try to make everything smaller and less exaggerated – everything!

Now when I walk into a room, I am very conscious about how much space I take up. Are my hands and arms open and outreaching? Do I lean in forward during discussions? When I sit are my legs tucked beneath me or boldly crossed in front of me? How can I expand my body when I'm interacting with people? What can I do to make them feel more comfortable, engage with them, and be intentional with my meaning?

Here's a trick. Spread your arms out like a bird. This expansion is your personal space and a big part of your physical presence. When you use this space, it has the energy and power that opens you out to others and causes them to react. It says "I am here, and I want to share with you something special!" I'm not telling you to walk into rooms with bird arms outstretched. There is nothing sexy about that. Just know that you have this circumference to move within as you engage with people. Think wider not tighter.

MAKE EYE CONTACT - ALWAYS

More than ever, a lack of eye contact is impacting all types of relationships and outcomes. Cell phones and computers have made it acceptable to have conversations without ever making direct eye contact. Creating a dynamic physical presence requires eye contact so put down those phones and tablets. There has been considerable research on how nonverbal cues, particularly those coming from the eyes, affects our behavior. One benefit is that eye-to-eye contact causes arousal. It's not just a sexual thing. When you are trying to get others passionate about your ideas eye-to-eye contact is crucial. People get excited on many levels by people AND ideas. Remember, you have moments to make an impact when meeting someone. Being shy or coy with your smile doesn't create a positive impact most of the time. It's less memorable. Why? Psychologist Paul Ekman has distinguished between smiles that represent genuine happiness ("Duchenne" smiles) and fake smiles that might be used to feign happiness, or cover some other emotion. The key to telling a fake smile from a real one is in the eyes. Real smiles with impact cause the eyes to narrow and create lines, or "crow's feet," at the outer corners. When smiling make sure your eyes are involved every time.

GROUND YOURSELF

Here is a strange story. I travel quite a bit and find myself with aching feet at the airport. On one particular trip, I paid for a 20-minute reflexology foot massage. The foot massage was so good it was almost orgasmic! At one point, the airport therapist asked me a question that hit me like a glass of cold water in the face.

Massage Therapist: Do you find it hard to hold your ground and stand with authority when talking to some people?

Me: Sometimes.

Massage Therapist: It's because you wear high heels, Miss.

Me: Huh? But I love the way my feet look in high heels. That's not going to change.

He then began to explain to me that high heels lifted my feet off the ground which stole from my physical gravitas. He told me that spending vast amounts of time in high heels kept me disconnected from the earth. I wanted to tell him to give it a rest, but I didn't want him to stop rubbing my feet - as he was and is still the best foot massage I ever experienced. So I let him continue.

He went on to tell me that without grounding our feet, we live too much in our heads (here is when it gets a little out there). When our feet are away from the solid ground too long, our inner critic voices begin to get louder. When I asked him what that all meant, he said this.

"Most women who wear high heels will stand with feet together, crossed over or with their weight on one foot only. They fidget. These postures mean you are not physically stable. Mentally you are not centered, and it makes you thrown off balance when faced with difficult questions or aggressive people."

He taught me an exercise that I did right there in the airport. I stood barefoot, feet flat on the ground, and pushed down with my feet. Eyes closed, I imagined thick roots pulling me towards the center of the earth as if I was planting myself there. He made me stand firmly planted for two minutes without speaking and eyes closed. When finished, I felt grounded. It is hard to explain, but you feel it. I also noticed that it changed how I stood; no more weight shifting, or crossed feet, or fidgeting.

Now, just before I go into a meeting, speak on stage, meet someone for the first time, or want to be taken seriously (even by my kids) I take two minutes to ground myself. You have to be barefoot, so I am constantly taking off my heels, but for me, it works every time.

CREATING A DYNAMIC AND POWERFUL PHYSICAL PRESENCE:

- Embracing and enjoying that you are a sexual being
- Highlighting the physical parts of your body you favor

- Detracting from the physical parts you don't
- Understanding how your body looks in clothing
- Being conscious of your whole package
- Making eye contact
- Appreciating other people's physicality
- Standing tall
- Taking up more space when interacting with people
- Grounding your body by planting your feet

Now can you see why just asking you to embrace your Boobs was easier – a shortcut of sorts to the bigger picture. It's about creating a dynamic and powerful physical presence that commands respect, allure, and loyalty. Admit you are a sexual being deserving of success in a man's world without giving up your divine feminine. Walk into a room and own it. Conduct a business meeting that is impactful, in your control and where you represent your most attractive self. Attract supporters in all your endeavors and create immediate connections in social settings, many times without ever saying a word. **It's all about how you walk into and exist in a room both physically and mentally with reverence for your physical being.**

Lesson Three: BALLS (Gambling on Yourself)

Massive success as a female entrepreneur requires you to believe with all your being that no matter what life throws at you – you've got the BALLS to handle it.

Joan Jett said, *"Girls have got balls. They are just a little higher up, that's all."* If you think about this for a moment, it makes total sense. But then there's Betty White who said, *"Why do people say 'grow some balls'? Balls are weak and sensitive. If you wanna be tough, grow a vagina. Those things can take a pounding."* She makes a fair point as well.

If the term Balls is offensive or off-putting to you because you think it is too masculine or impolite, then I would ask you to consider the alternatives.

The crass literal translation to *" he's got balls bigger than Texas"* is *'She's got a Vagina bigger than Texas'*. What woman on the planet wants to be thought of as having an expansive vagina? Or what about 'he had big balls so he succeeded' translating into 'she had big boobs so she succeeded'. See, it doesn't work. It just doesn't have the same oomph! Can we agree on this? In this case, borrowing terms from the guys is more appropriate. Here are reasons why.

Ladies, we do technically have balls. We have two ovaries (our birthing center) which we carry on the inside, and they perform a similar function as male testicles. So, let's embrace the term 'grow some balls' with a little more fun.

Having balls is not just about having self-confidence. It's not simply about being brave or taking chances. It means that you take 100% ownership for the outcome of your decisions. It means you believe in your intelligence, expertise, talent, and fortitude enough that taking risks is not an obstacle. To be successful as an entrepreneur you have to believe that you can get yourself out of any situation. You have to believe so much in your intelligence, emotional strength, determination and creativity that you are willing to take risks. Risk-taking is not optional. A quote that inspires me:

"Do one thing every day that scares you." – Eleanor Roosevelt

Many women are putting this quote into action. For example, Elle Kaplan, founder of LexION Capital was quoted as saying, "I was called crazy, and people laughed at my face when I announced I was leaving Wall Street to form my own company. It was outlandish enough for a woman to be an executive in finance, but considered absolutely nuts to own your own firm. I also had absolutely no funding to back my company, so I was risking everything by starting LexION Capital." That's ballsy. (Do you feel better about the word when I add a 'y'?)

I search for stories about women who blend their personal and professional life, like Maya Brenner, founder of Maya Brenner Designs. She admitted this, "After having my second baby, I needed to do something drastic to be able to be a mom and run my successful jewelry business. I wanted to make more money for less work. So, after almost ten years of selling wholesale through a sales rep and trade shows and being in top stores such as Anthropologie, Henri Bendel, and Fred Segal, I decided to stop selling to stores and focus primarily on selling retail on my own website. It was a huge risk, but worth it. When a celebrity wore my jewelry, or my designs were featured in a magazine, my website was credited instead of other stores." Her risk paid off.

True entrepreneurial women are not interested in the ordinary. We desire the extraordinary. And when we decide to bet on ourselves that is what we get out of every experience.

An example of a calculated gamble is the career path of Lisi Harrison, author of the ultra-successful Monster High books. During her 12 years at MTV, she continued to pursue her passion for writing and becoming an author. She left MTV to launch her book series. She has this to say, "This is our big chance to see what people think of us. The real us. We have to show them there's nothing to be afraid of. If we don't get over our fears, they never will." She had to believe completely that birthing her book series would pay off bigger than her secure job at MTV. She had the balls to bet on it.

When I lost my scholarship in college, I had two choices: quit or pay for it myself. I came up with a big gamble. I would stay enrolled at full tuition and figure out how to pay my way for six months while I applied for the next round of financial aid. I would either succeed or fail.

When I decided to move to Maine with a boy I had known three months with nothing to fall back on I was gambling on true love.

When I decided to start a business with a newborn on my lap and grow it to twice the size with each new pregnancy, it wasn't because I knew what to expect but rather because I believed that having a family was worth the risk.

When I walked away from a million-dollar job offer with no more than $1000 in the bank it was because I was betting on myself to earn more on my terms one day.

When my attorney begged me to file bankruptcy, and I refused, it wasn't because I knew how to avoid it. I decided it was against my Core drivers and would rather chance that I could earn my way out of it.

How did I develop "balls the size of Texas"? Simple. I spent a long time gambling with other people's balls and losing.

You can create a list of family members, close friends, lovers, and business partners that have let you down, left you hanging, abandoned you in your time of need, or worse, tried to keep you down. Sad but true. Why put your faith in others to help you out in your darkest hour – some will and others won't. Why gamble on them? **You just have to look in the mirror and say "I have the balls to do this."** Each time you take a risk, your balls get bigger, and future risk is less daunting. The more we gamble on ourselves, the more extraordinary things will happen in all areas of our life. It's all a gamble. Gamble on your own balls – never theirs.

What do you do with your Brains, Boobs, and Balls now that you know what they stand for?

Become uncomfortable.

Become unrealistic.

Lesson Four begins now!

Lesson Four: Be the Unrealistic Saleswoman

As a female entrepreneur, you must become the Unrealistic Saleswoman to sell your vision of the future to yourself, your family and those in business. You must gain their support long before your vision becomes a reality.

To change your world, you must throw reality out of the window! Your vision is only unrealistic because it hasn't happened yet. Those around you may say it's a 'dumb idea' and even withhold support. That's just because you haven't sold them on the finished product.

Your current reality is the sum of the decisions you've made up until this moment based on existing beliefs and thoughts. When you become unrealistic about your life, you can change your reality.

You've heard the phrase 'dream big.' Dreaming isn't enough. Big dreams are not enough. Many people dream big and then wonder why nothing happens. Nothing happens as a result of small and safe actions based on a situational reality. Nothing happens because you haven't sold that dream to yourself much less those in the community that could help you get there.

You alone can envision your desired future. When you hear those around you say 'you have to be realistic' it means two things. First, you are playing it too safe to begin with, or they would be saying 'I can't believe you are doing this.' Take bolder action. It's scary but it'll get you places being realistic will not. And second, you are doing a terrible job at selling your vision to people. You have to sell it! Sell it till they buy it! You can't create a business if no one sees the value. In business, your idea is worthless unless someone pays for it. The naysayers will forget all the reasons you can't do something when they have to swallow your passionate, consistent, and self-believed sales pitch. All great entrepreneurs are salespeople gifted at generating buy-in from those around them. In business, you have to sell every day.

What about outside of business? You can't ask for support from your family and friends unless they believe in your unrealistic plans. You cannot build your dream life alone – you need the support of others. You must be as much a saleswoman in your personal life as you are a dreamer, entrepreneur, mother, wife, or friend.

Start with yourself. The thought of tackling the success of your business, family and sex life all at the same time probably seems daunting, maybe even overwhelming. You had better start selling yourself on the benefits of having success in every area of your life now. Once you've got your pitch down, you need to turn to your spouse, partner, kids, family, and friends and see if they buy your unrealistic ideas. If not, change your pitch, get more enthusiastic and sell them on why being unrealistic in your actions now will generate a better outcome… soon. Here is the easiest example I can give you.

You are building a business that is all consuming, on a tight budget, in a relationship that is already over-taxed, and you are juggling debt. The reality is, now is not the right time to have a baby. Your partner agrees – how could you possibly handle a baby now with a business and not enough money? So, you, your partner, and your life circumstances all concur – it's not the time to have a baby! Then you wake up one morning pregnant unexpectedly. Even you were dutifully taking your birth control pill.

The lesson: Don't get stuck in your reality because life will throw a wrench it in anyway. Instead, take responsibility and create your own reality. This is how my first child came into the picture.

WRITING YOUR UNREALISTIC FAIRYTALE INTO REALITY

Having a baby. Falling in love. Starting a business. Buying a house. Investing. Inventing a product. It doesn't matter which one. Your ideas must come from a place of 'making it work' not from a list of reasons on why 'it can't work'. Start by telling yourself the fairytale you desire.

Grab a pen and paper and write it down. Or just fill in the blanks below to get your mind started. Write down the story of how you can have what you want right now that fits in with your current reality, time-starved relationship, and money-tight bank account. The process almost writes itself.

What is it you want in your life right now that you don't have: the job, the lover, the baby, the bank account, the time off, the invention, the healed relationship, the right number on the scale, the education, etc. Be specific:

_____

_____

_____

_____

Now write down all the ways you could incorporate these things into your daily life today – **even if it seems unrealistic.** If you have to, add magic into your storyline to open up possibilities. As that fairytale becomes more and more unrealistic add back details that make it possible – even if you have no idea how to accomplish these details right now.

_____

_____

_____

_____

As you develop your story, it should read like a fairytale. Have fun with it while you are being unrealistically specific in what you create.

'Once upon a time, there was a woman who wanted it all away even when it seemed like the completely wrong time...'

Once you have written down the story and it excites you – it's time to share it. Retell your story full of excitement and passion to your partner, a friend, or anyone you trust. Each time a 'reality block' is

mentioned by the other person, counter it with a very specific reason why it doesn't have to be this way.

Write down these 'reality blocks' and how you think you get around them – even if it unrealistic right now.

_____

_____

_____

_____

_____

_____

_____

_____

_____

_____

_____

_____

_____

_____

_____

_____

_____

If the person can't see/understand this new reality you are trying to "birth" then you need to rework your sales pitch – starting with your own buy-in.

Remember, you can't sell (or bring into reality) what you don't truly buy into yourself.

Think about how you become unrealistic about your business, your personal life, and your family life. What are the possibilities you can dream up?

"Charlie, the reality is your business is a long shot – the road is too steep for you to make it realistically." If I had accepted this statement when my banker, tax attorney and employees said it to me years ago, you would not be reading this book today. The more they told me I was being unrealistic about avoiding bankruptcy, the more it occurred to me that my only solution was to invent a new reality.

I spent a week of sleepless nights convincing myself that I could resurrect my business from a four million dollar debt-grave. Every morning, with deep bags under my eyes, I told my husband my latest plans for transforming my business until one morning he said, "Sounds like you can do this." Selling this un-birthed reality to attorneys and bankers was not that easy. They built their careers on being realistic. So, when my unrealistic story of how I would pull through didn't convince them, I tried again. This time with spreadsheets. When the spreadsheets had holes poked through them, I tried creating different revenue models for them to get excited about. To convince the banks and attorneys that I could earn my way out of a four-million-dollar hole I had to become unrealistic and sell the intangible. Even if they couldn't see how I was going earn more revenue, they could see my passion, my commitment, and the crazy look when they told me it couldn't be done! **I made them understand that I saw something they couldn't.** It was a big gamble. My personal assets would be used as ante in this round of betting. If I couldn't make it happen my family lost everything. Ultimately, I sold the bank on my unrealistic vision when I said, "Give me four months to hit these revenue markers and if I can't do it - I'll shut it down, but if I can do it you are going to give me another six months to do it again. And then another six months after that until you can see my plan is solid." I sold them on four months of life-line, and that was enough for me to bring my unrealistic ideas into reality.

I challenge you to be unrealistic in what you expect from yourself, business, personal relationships and your sex life too.

Part Two

All the Dirty Details

We like to pretend that our generous impulses come naturally. But the reality is we often become our kindest, most ethical selves only by seeing what it feels like to be a selfish jackass first. It's the reason we have to get burned before we understand the power of fire; the reason our most meaningful relationships are so often those that continued beyond the very juncture at which they came the closest to ending.

— *Cheryl Strayed,*
Tiny Beautiful Things: Advice on Love and Life from Dear Sugar

---

Chapter Two

At the Beginning There Was Stupidity and Sex

Did I mean to become a CEO or an entrepreneur? No! I was following a boy from Boston to Maine because I had read on *On the Road* by Jack Kerouac and was smitten by this quote:

"The only people for me are the mad ones, the ones who are mad to live, mad to talk, mad to be saved, desirous of everything at the same time, the ones who never yawn or say a commonplace thing, but burn, burn, burn like fabulous yellow roman candles exploding like spiders across the stars."

The passion in that quote so deeply resonates with me... but I digress again. Let's instead start behind Fenway Park.

When I auditioned for the College of Fine Arts at Boston University, I had no hopes of actually getting accepted as one of the 64 incoming freshmen to the elite program. I was a poor kid from the San Fernando Valley, who thought she was cursed with bad fortune – I was not chosen for things like this. Nor did I ever imagine I would be granted a nearly full scholarship including room and board. My father was so proud because all I had talked about since I was five was becoming an actress and now I was attending one of the best schools in the country for this pursuit. My future lay ahead. Boston University was alive with possibilities. I arrived with one suitcase and $400. Despite my desire to be at Boston University, after my first year I was deeply unsatisfied. I didn't know exactly why but studying the art of acting all day was not what I expected it to be, and I became restless and distracted.

The head of the department reminded me that the program cut students every semester based on performance; my graduating class would go from 64 to under 20 as the semesters went on. I was not on the cut list yet, but the department recognized my detachment.

"If you aren't serious about your future with the program it is selfish to hold one of the other students back – there is only so much room."

I tried to re-engage myself. I wanted to act and one day become a director, so succeeding in this University was my first step.

Then one day, after a four-hour long method acting class where I had to roll around the floor pretending to be a Cocaine junkie, I simply fell out of love entirely with my future as an actress. I wanted to direct documentaries, not act. I left the class and went straight to the University office where I filled out the forms to change my major to Communications. Getting a degree in Communications would help me raise money for my documentaries – that was my rationale. It took me forty-five minutes to fill out the paperwork and twenty-five minutes to reregister for classes in the College of Communications. It took seven days for the letter to arrive at my campus apartment stating that I had one week to move out and three weeks before my tuition needed to be paid.

"Ms. Moss, I understand that you were unaware your scholarship package was linked to your admittance into the School of Fine Arts. Your scholarship was based on your audition. When you made the decision to transfer colleges you revoked your scholarship, and they have since filled your spot in the program. The next time you make such a big decision, I'd suggest you do some research first."

AT THE BEGINNING THERE WAS STUPIDITY...

Making decisions is the easy part. Sticking to the decision after it becomes a reality – a tough reality since your decision was ill thought out - that's where things get dicey.

I was in total shock! I felt plain stupid – I didn't read the fine print, and I had essentially destroyed the life I had been working toward all four years in high school. Was my only option to go home, attend a State school, and start over? Hadn't I just escaped from my life at home?

As I let the situation take root in my mind, I kept coming back to the same set of thoughts. I won't let my family find out. I can't go backward. The truth was that even if I wanted to go home, I couldn't afford to – I was flat broke. So were my parents. I needed to depend only on myself. So I started running... running to keep up... to stay ahead... to avoid danger... to escape going backward... it would be years before I would stop and catch my breath.

I already had a job at Kinko's Copy Shop but it didn't pay nearly enough to go to school and live on my own. I needed more money that I could earn around my class schedule. I began to walk the streets of Boston looking for any signs that said 'Now Hiring.' Within 72 hours I had secured a weekend job as a cage dancer at an eighteen plus night club behind Fenway Park. I saw the Help Wanted sign when I was looking for a room to rent on the same side of the street. All the job required was that I wear a skimpy outfit and dance in a cage in the center of the dance floor from 11 pm to 1 am. No stripping. No touching. I was forbidden to take the bikini outfit off .

The club was where students from MIT, Boston University, Boston College and Emerson would come to every week to blow off steam. My job was to encourage people to dance longer so they would buy more drinks and stay later. Each night I worked with three other girls for a total of four cages spread out all over the dance floor. It paid $50 cash per night. I could keep any tips I was passed inside the cage as long as there was no touching.

The manager was willing to overlook the fact that I wasn't old enough to work in the club in lieu of my chest size. I started working the same night because one of the other girls had an extra outfit. As I put on the neon pink, size-too-small, Lycra one-piece napkin I compartmentalized my emotions into a box in my brain called 'Deal with THIS Feeling Later' and I mentally prepared myself to step inside the cage.

I am squeezing into a used cage-girl costume. Did she wash it? Please God! Is it on backward? How can you tell? What if someone recognizes me? Now I know why God gave me big boobs so I could pay my way through college in a pink napkin! Hold it together, Charlie, you need enough for a down payment on the room the 40-year old, hairy, scary drummer down the street is offering. I need the apartment... it's just two doors down from here and four blocks from my old campus room. It's like I'll still be living on campus. Just a few nights a week pays my rent. You've got this! God, please let her have washed the pink Band-Aid please...

Going to school full time, working five days a week at Kinko's and cage dancing three nights a week was an incredible juggling act that still wasn't enough for tuition, food, rent, and books. I had limited time to figure it out before I was kicked out of school for non-payment. Then, I met a girl in the entrance way of my apartment building behind Fenway Park. She was attending MIT across the river and had also opted to sublet a room inside this building– her roommate was a 75-year-old retired machinist who was a die-hard Red Socks fan. Her story was only similar to mine in that she was putting herself through school.

Her father had wanted her to work in the family business and, when she refused, she was on her own for college. Her name was Karin, she had just turned 20 and was determined to be a lawyer. There was an immediate connection between this 5'0 foot Korean Sorority chick and my 5'10 Mexican self. It led to a rapid-fire question and answer exchange.

How are your grades? Will you get enough from student loans next semester to quit one of your jobs? Do you tell anyone where you live? Did you know you can get 15 Top Ramen Noodle Soups and a jar of Ragu for $4.00 at the liquor store near the laundry mat?

When I asked her how she was making enough money to pay for MIT she explained, like me, she had two other jobs during the day and had taken out some loans. She was currently on her way to her night job three doors down behind Fenway Park on the same side of the street as the night club. It was a private business run out of an apartment. This company was an emerging Chat Line run by a very entrepreneurial 27-year-old MIT Engineering Major name Raj. Karin's job was to keep lonely gentlemen on the line talking for more than 10 minutes at a time. Sometimes it got weird. Sometimes it was XXX. Sometimes it was corny. Sometimes the callers didn't even talk back. Sometimes the men were just depressed, which made it a drag. But the time went by fast, and Raj paid in cash. She highly recommended I gave it a shot.

Two days later I was auditioning for Raj in the kitchen of his apartment just doors away from my rented room. His living room had nine phones plugged into the walls with another four plugged into his bedroom. He hired me that same day, and I had five 12- minute-long phone calls my first night. He handed me $140 in cash.

Within three weeks I had been nicknamed 29 by the girls because I was averaging twenty-nine minutes on the phone with lonely souls in Boston who preferred a Chat Line over real human interaction. Raj was thrilled because he made money on ten-minute calls; there was a nice profit which he shared at $25 extra for every twenty-nine- minute call, so I told myself I was a highly paid actress. This made it easier for me to forget how I was putting myself through college.

Three jobs with tips plus selling most of my clothes and dorm room furniture allowed me to pay for one semester as I applied for financial aid. I was able to get 21 credits worth of classes to fit into two and a half days allowing me to work the three jobs each week. I lived on Top Ramen.

On several nights, walking home from the club, wearing a small bikini underneath a winter coat I had borrowed, I had to out run men following me down the street. Being locked in a strange apartment with eight other girls, talking to desperate men all over Boston, about things much sadder, depressing, and weirder than sex could have easily ended with my disappearance. I would fall asleep in class with a tape recorder going so I could listen to the lectures on the train to Kinko's. Then, falling asleep on the train while listening to the lectures, I risked being mugged on the way home from Kinko's at midnight. All of these things were my normal.

There are friends that I still have today that were nearby me during this period of my life in Boston who will read this part of the story and ask, 'Why didn't you ask me for help?' Good question.

I was so focused on graduating from Boston University the way my father and I had planned that my twenty-hour long days seemed like the only way. My actions were desperate, and I was not proud of them. I had convinced myself that I was *living through my decision* to graduate college in Boston. This was before I understood that there were different ways to live through a decision.

AT THE BEGINNING THERE WAS ALSO SEX...

Just when the reality of my situation started to feel too heavy, I met a boy. Not just any boy. He was in his last semester at Boston University getting his Masters of Fine Arts in Theater, and he was everything I never knew I wanted in life. After three months of dating, he told me he had been offered a job in Maine at a very prestigious theater right after he graduated. Would I consider moving to Maine with him?

I was two semesters away from graduating, hopelessly in debt, exhausted from working so much, guilt-ridden from lying to my family about my situation, and overall deflated by how my life was turning out. More importantly, I was irrationally head over heels in love with this boy.

I was very torn. I was two quick semesters away from a diploma from Boston University that would be worth something. If I kept my head down, I was smart enough with enough hard work in me to do it. I also knew that with this boy my spirit was truly happy, and that was the stuff of great poetry. Would I ever find this happiness again if I didn't go to Maine? It never occurred to me that graduating any college would have probably been an alternate option. Why? I had been raised never to quit. I had been raised always to follow through with what I said I would do. I was proud. I was scared. I didn't ask for help. I didn't understand ME yet.

That night I sat in a deli on Commonwealth Avenue feeling numb; paralyzed by wanting to make the right decision without regret or mistake. Coming from a broken household one thing I knew I wanted more than anything was to find the love of my life and make a great family. The boy was a risk on every level. Staying in Boston was tedious, but the risks I could calculate.

How Did I Decide To Leave Boston?

I was watching Alice in Wonderland on TV in a deli eating a cold Knish. Remember this scene between Alice and the Cheshire cat?

Alice asked the Cheshire cat, who was sitting in a tree, "What road do I take?"

The cat asked, "Where do you want to go?" "I don't know," Alice answered.

"Then," said the cat, "it really doesn't matter, does it?"

—*Lewis Carroll, Alice's Adventures in Wonderland*

So I followed the sex.

Lesson Five: Core Drivers

To be wildly successful you must clearly identify your Core Drivers and commit to the WHY behind them. It guides your choices, actions, and feelings for the best possible outcome.

As entrepreneurs, parents, lovers, or global community members Core Drivers are the first and most important obligations in our life that keep us physically, mentally, and spiritually whole. They are ongoing, non-negotiable commitments to our self. Core Drivers are sacred decisions about how we want to exist in this world above all else. They make up our being, drive our decisions and create internal happiness and peace. **Your Core Drivers (and the WHY behind them) have to be so big and so important that you will never give up on them.** You will not always be able to see clearly what you're creating but with a strong sense WHY you are doing it, you can be confident the rest will work out. When things blow up in your face, it won't matter because you believe so deeply in your Core Drivers, that you decide to try again and again until you get it right. Not every decision we make is the right one. Not every decision gets us ahead. But every decision should be motivated by our Core Drivers.

Below is a partial, in no particular order, list of my Core Drivers:

1. **Stay Connected to God in Physical Action**
2. **Follow Love Not Security**
3. **Follow Passion Not Success**
4. **Follow Abundance with the Intent to Share It**
5. **Be Kind**
6. **Marry and Stay Married Happily - Forever**
7. **Raise my Children without a Nanny**

8. Inspire my Children by Example
9. Give my Children a Premium Education
10. Always be My Own Boss
11. Take Risks in Everything
12. Keep my Extended Family Close Knit
13. Artistically Create Stuff Daily
14. Fall Madly in Love Often with People and Ideas
15. Create Opportunity for Others Despite Personal Status
16. Do Things that Scare Me
17. Don't Engage in Negative Actions
18. Always Have Pets
19. Create Wealth
20. Never Lose My Vanity

Moving to Maine after knowing a boy for only three months definitely falls under a Core Driver. *Follow Love not Security.*

UNDERSTANDING YOUR WHYS

To create a Core Driver list, we need to understand our Whys? Great questions to ask:

- Why does it all matter?
- Why am I doing what I'm doing?
- Why am I hesitating?
- Why do I love what I love and hate what I hate?
- Why is it never enough?
- Why haven't I pursued my passion?
- Why haven't I achieved the success I know I am capable?
- Why am I always distracted?
- Why do I feel incomplete?
- Why can't I feel spiritually connected?

When you list your answers out honestly – on a piece of paper – you will begin to see similarities in your answers, your WHYs. These similarities point the direction to your Core Drivers.

The WHY behind the Core Driver is the gasoline that fuels decisions. Making decisions without understanding the WHY is like driving a car without knowing how big the gas tank is, how much gas is left in the tank, or where the next gas station is.

I used to drive through life putting my decisions in lanes: the good lane (it feels safe and comforting), the bad lane (it feels irresponsible or dangerous), the carpool lane (it feels like a compromise), and the exit lane (make uncomfortable feelings stop). I used to make decisions based on logic. Based on fear. Based on empathy. Based on exhaustion.

Making decisions is the most important thing you CAN do to live life on your terms. My system of decision making requires that I put my actions and decisions into three categories:

DEFINING YOUR CORE DRIVERS

These are decisions that define you in every way. Things like:

- **The type of parent you want to be:** (ex. stay-at-home, working parent, single parent)
- **The type of work that fulfills you:** (ex. focused career, a job that affords you free time, a job that fuels your creative pursuits, an inventor, owning your company)
- **The type of personal relationship you desire:** (ex. marriage, gay, lesbian, bi-sexual, life partner, or multiple lovers)
- **Your spirituality:** (ex. actively involved in a church, atheist, committed to deepening your spiritual connection)
- **What will ultimately fuel your Soul:** (ex. becoming and artist, writing, travel, going into politics, developing your own product, having children, becoming famous, leaving a mark, finding a soul mate)

ACTIVATING DECISIONS

When you make Activating Decisions, you are trying to get closer to achieving or maintaining your Core Drivers. Activating Decisions are made daily, weekly, or as needed. For example, if your Core Driver is to be your own boss then quitting your job would be the Activating Decision you make; giving you more time to build your business. Examples of others:

- eliminating birth control to start a family
- going to marriage counseling to save your marriage
- singing on a public stage to cure stage fright
- going into Rehab to get off of drugs
- enrolling in college courses at night to finish your degree
- going to the gym every day to maintain your health

Activating Decisions aren't always right for your circumstances. Activating Decisions should support your Core Drivers and change when they take you in the wrong direction. As I reveal my story, you will be able to see how one Activating Decision led to another and another until I was making actual progress in all areas of my life.

BALANCING DECISIONS

Balancing Decisions help you stay balanced when an Activating Decision turns out wrong. They help keep you in place, intact, or in the game, while you make new Activating Decisions. For example, let's say a Core Driver is to start your own business, so you directionally decide to quit your job and invest all your time and money into your new business. You then get off to a slow start and financially cannot support yourself without another source of income. Rather than give up on your Core Driver you make a Balancing Decision to get a part-time job or take out a loan. This does not move you closer to having your own successful business. It does allow you to keep trying to build your own business without going broke. Your Balancing Decision keeps you afloat while you change directions and seek a new path to your Core Driver. Another Balancing Decision could be joining a social group after a bad breakup to keep your mindset on finding love rather than losing it.

Create your Core Driver List, then start making choices about how you're going to support these Core Drivers in your business, family, and personal life! Once you identify your unique Core Driver, making decisions, and sticking with those decisions, becomes easier, and you feel in control of your journey.

Don't hesitate to make decisions. Sometimes making a DAMN decision is the only friend a girl's got.

My Core Drivers:

1. _____
2. _____
3. _____
4. _____
5. _____

Activating Decisions:

1. _____
2. _____
3. _____
4. _____
5. _____

Balancing Decisions:

1. _____

2. _____

3. _____

4. _____

5. _____

Chapter Three

CEO by Accidental Choice

A forty-one-inch bust and a lot of perseverance will get you more than a cup of coffee- a lot more.
—*Jayne Mansfield*
(on screen legend appearing in twenty-nine movies, a musician and comedienne. Her I.Q. was reputed to be 163. She was the mother of five.)

LIVING WITH MY BOSTON DECISION

I never intended to be a CEO. It was sort of an accidental choice; the result of making an Activating Decision about my future after realizing the Activating Decision to move to Boston was not fulfilling me. Let me explain.

Everything seemed to be going my way in Maine. I graduated from the University of Southern Maine in one semester, not two. I had a good job. When he was not at the theater I had a great boyfriend. I had even started making friends. Again I found myself restless and distracted.

One evening, after sitting in front of the TV waiting for him to come home from the theater, I realized I was covering up a new kind of unhappiness that I thought came from my relationship with the boy. He had moved to Maine to undertake a career opportunity that allowed him to work with some of the best directors and designers in the theater world. He was very committed to our relationship, but his success in the theater depended on his time being dedicated there first. I was barely 21 while he was nearing 30. When I wanted to go dancing all night, he wanted to lay low. He was at a different level in his career and had different life goals. I felt secondary. I began to resent it. My resentment turned into arguments. Arguments turned into silence. Silence turned into indifference. My decision to start a life with this boy in Maine began to feel like the worst decision I could have made. I knew true love was a Core Driver of mine, but I also knew that love shouldn't be this hard or make me feel this alone.

I turned off the TV, packed my bags, and sat on the edge of the bed waiting for him to come home. I rehearsed my exit speech.

I'm moving back to Boston to start over. I need to be with people my own age. I need a social life. I need to work a job in the field I want to end up in. We are in different places. Things just aren't working out. We tried.

As I heard the key turn in the lock and his footsteps down the hallway, electrical shocks hit my gut so sharply they almost knocked me off the bed. I can't put it into words the feeling, but it was deep and desperate. I know now that back then I was trying to make an Activating Decision that would take me away from my Core Driver of *following love, not security*. My body knew it even if my mind had not caught up yet. It was a gut reaction I could not ignore despite my logic. I quickly hid the bags under the bed, and when he walked in the room, I put on a huge smile. He smiled back.

"I brought home Chinese!"

That night gave me my first clue to why I was unhappy. The problem wasn't that he wasn't spending enough time with me. I wasn't spending enough time *on me*. His life and career were moving faster than mine.

I was essentially bored and frustrated by my own lack of action. I had become complacent because I was no longer struggling to make ends meet like I was in Boston. I was not creating anything new or going anywhere different. That was my fault, not a flaw in our relationship. I had taken a leap of faith moving to Maine with him and expected my faith to take care of the rest. I had no real plan when I left Boston other than finishing school. I was suffering from the 'Now What Blues.' As we put the last Chinese food container in the fridge, I told myself that this boy was worth my commitment. I decided that I would be happy about our relationship while I fixed my personal unhappiness.

ACTION WITHOUT CLEAR DIRECTION

The next day I walked into my boss's office and said, "Why don't you put your radio interviews on TV and sell the products that way?" He said that he had no experience in TV. I explained to him that I had plenty of experience in developing TV and video from college. I could put his radio shows on TV for much less than he thought. It was the ultimate white lie. To my surprise, he gave me a budget and told me to go for it.

When I came home that night, I was outside of my body with excitement. I was going to produce my very own TV infomercial with my very own budget.

The boy said, "You know how to do that?"

And then it hit me. Nope! I had no idea how to do it. I let my stomach do flips for one minute before I responded, "Not exactly but I can figure it out!"

For the next six months, it was the boy who never saw me as I threw every ounce of my being into producing this TV infomercial with my limited budget and knowledge. I left for work at six in the morning and sometimes did not return until after midnight. I worked seven days a week trying to gather all the pieces I needed to make this a success. I watched other infomercials on TV all day long from the office. I took calls in the call center so I could hear what customers would say about the products they had heard about on the radio. I interviewed every production company in Maine until I found one that would work within our budget. I spent hours in the editing bay second guessing my editorial choices. And I held my breath the day the TV infomercial aired for the first time. Every fiber of my being felt alive. I was a TV producer!

Don't Get Too Settled In

"Will you marry me?"

The answer was yes! We would be leaving Maine for his new job in New Jersey as a Professor of Theater. My boss eagerly allowed me to work from a home office in New Jersey rather than have me quit. We were having too much success on TV to interrupt things now. So the decision to marry and move seemed easy. Decisions often seem easy.

Living With My New Jersey Decision

Once in New Jersey, my boss had me traveling all over the country. I was home only two weeks out of the month. The boy, now my husband Tom, was happy to allow me the freedom to grow this new career, while he dove into his new life in academia. I was even pursuing my own Master's Degree in Publishing from New York University.

My first infomercial was a hit! It was a bigger than big hit – generating the company millions in sales. After the initial success of the first project, my boss allowed me to produce three other TV infomercials and all the new radio infomercials. I was very busy and for a while very happy. Then life got in the way... again.

I got pregnant 'on the pill.' The conversation in my head started.

Does Tom have super sperm? Or am I super fertile? We can't afford a baby! What about NYU? I can't travel to New York with a baby? We have no room for a baby. I'm such a slut. What? I'm married now. I can be pregnant. I shouldn't be pregnant. Now I'm going to be a fat, stay at home mom and

Tom will have an affair because… because why? I can be one of those skinny pregnant women and lose the baby weight I'm only 24! I can't afford to get my Masters and have a baby. This is like Boston all over again except I'll be wearing an apron in a South Jersey diner instead of a pink Lycra napkin in a sweaty night club. I wonder what Tom will say… I was on the pill dammit!

Tom was, of course, over the moon about my pregnancy. After my initial mental freak out, I knew I was incredibly happy I was going to be a mother. Being that it was my first child and I traveled so frequently, I was able to keep my pregnancy a secret until I was a whole seven months along. By this time, I had produced several more hit infomercials for the company, and I was signing one client after another on their behalf. There was no reason that I didn't deserve a big promotion. I had earned my place in the company big belly and all.

I approached my boss respectfully about the promotion, hoping that it would be enough to raise a family on and allow me to stop traveling as much. I hadn't told him about the baby. I wanted the discussion to be focused on my merits. When he told me that I was responsible for much of the company's success but that I was already making more than everyone else in the company and a promotion was "premature", I swallowed hard. A lump began to form on the top of my head from hitting it so hard on the glass ceiling.

I was mad. Furious to be honest. He knew I was the reason his radio company had turned into one of the larger TV infomercial companies in the small span of three years. He also believed that I owed him for the opportunity "to learn the business on his dime."

Raj had said this exact same thing to me the day I told him I couldn't work the Chat Line anymore- "oh you learned how to make money on my dime now you're too good for the work?" I have never thought that I should get special consideration as a woman but to hear that I was being "allowed to learn on their dime" made me feel small and insignificant.

For a moment, I thought about just getting a TV producer job in New Jersey, but I knew one thing for sure: I was in a man's industry, and there was no room for my growing belly. I let my boss's comments settle in my head. It planted a Core Driver so deep inside me: I needed to find a way to control my own net worth.

MAKING A DEFINITIVE DECISION

I swallowed hard again. I knew this was a fight I wouldn't win and, unlike that day on the bridge with Daniel Harp, I had no desire to fight back. It wasn't worth the fight. I thanked my boss for the opportunity and told him that I would be moving on to start my own production company. I hoped he would consider being my first client. Surprised and with few words, he shook my hand.

When I relayed the story to Tom and my father-in-law on the drive home from Maine to Boston where we were staying for the weekend, both were surprised I had made the decision so quickly. My father-in-law asked me, "Do you know how to run a production company?" My answer was the same as before. I can figure it out.

I could feel the weight of the deep breath Tom and his father took while trying to decide what to say next. It was his father who spoke first. "Well, if you're going to do this, then I should help you get started. You will need some seed money to get a computer and things. I'm going to give you five thousand dollars to get the company going, and we'll see where it goes, okay."

"Wow! That is so very generous, but I can't accept your money. I can do this on my own."

"I don't doubt that you can young lady, but that's my grandchild in there. Consider the money an advance on the baby's college fund."

My father-in-law is Italian. You don't argue with an Italian grandfather-to-be. I was now irrevocably involved in the Mafia. The Italian Grandfather Mafia. His money came with grandchild strings. **I was literally giving up my first born child to start my business!**

This is how I accidentally chose to begin my career as a CEO and Entrepreneur – with decisive action and no real plan.

WHAT IF...

If I had never moved to Maine and followed that boy is a pivotal question in my life. It was in Maine that I discovered the industry I work in today. It was in Maine that I finished my degree while working jobs I could be proud of. It was in Maine I married the boy who became the father of the most amazing children I could ever dream up. And it was in Maine that I developed the courage to become an entrepreneur. Being happy has always been more important to me than financial security. **It was my unhappiness in Boston when introduced to the potential promise of happiness with the boy that sparked the fire in my gut... to take *uncomfortable action.***

Lesson Six: Laugh to Insure Happiness

There is only one reason to be happy in life – because you choose to be. Happiness is a choice. You can't be happy if you are not laughing!

At any given moment there are 100+ reasons to be upset, depressed, angry, hurt, and hopeless and all those other non-Hallmark greeting card emotions. Or you can choose happiness. We know we have one shot to make life extraordinary. Entrepreneurs are, in some ways, hard coded not be naturally happy. We excel in risk and fear situations. We become unsatisfied easily because our vision is always evolving. A state of happy doesn't always work for us even though it is where we will excel. This is why you must always be looking for a good belly laugh because it is the fastest way to ignite happiness.

Seriously, to be holistically successful in anything you do, you need to develop a great sense of humor. Without it, choosing happiness becomes harder and harder. On this entrepreneurial road, you will walk through long stretches where you are not satisfied; you may be frustrated, course corrections will need to be made, fear, jealousy, or anger will flare up, and you will need to make different choices. This will always be the case. You must make the conscious choice to seek out the funny part of every situation to bring the happiness forward.

LET'S GET DIRECT AND PERSONAL

- If you're in a marriage that is unhappy or unfulfilling but you're settling for it – thinking it's the best it is going to get – you're wrong. You're holding yourself back. You're cheating your family. You're blaming the wrong person. You're being unkind and selfish. Trying to bring happiness back into your marriage seems too difficult, so settling becomes the direction. Happiness in your marriage is your choice and responsibility.

- If you're in a relationship that is not making you happy but you justify it by saying "it'll get better" – you're lying to yourself. Being in love should not be hard if it is the right kind. Don't be afraid to acknowledge when it is time to move on – no matter how scary.

- If you justify not being in a relationship by thinking, "I just haven't met anyone worthwhile yet" – look in the mirror. If you are living life waiting for the right person to find you, then you are asking to be alone. Happiness reflects happiness. If you are living every day with joy, then you will undoubtedly attract others in the right way.

- If you have shut out family members because they make you unhappy, take a moment to rethink your role in the family. Holding familial grudges drains you of productive energy. When possible, find a way to add them back into your life. Have a sense of humor about your relationship with them and make the rest work.

- If you're unhappy because of the way you look or your weight isn't where it should be, understand these are physical manifestations of an internal unhappiness. You need to get off your butt and change. Stop making excuses that only hold you back.

- If your job makes you unhappy, you are not doing it right or you don't belong there. Work harder for better results and rewards or quit and move on. Stop wasting everyone's time.

- If you go through the day and just suddenly feel blue, detached, or stressed, it is because of the things you choose to think about. You have the power to change your thoughts instantly.

Look, I'm not asking everyone to wave a lighter in the air and start singing campfire songs. Happiness doesn't come easily; it takes work. If you don't have a sense of humor about life and all the crap it throws your way, AVOID getting married, forget about having kids, and give up on having your own business! You cannot survive these things unless you can laugh about all the problems they will cause in your life.

When everything is going well, being happy is simple. But when we're facing challenges and uncertainty, it takes conscious effort to avoid going into "victim mode".

As Eckhart Tolle says: "The primary cause of unhappiness is never the situation but your thoughts about it."

Similarly, Buddhist wisdom teaches us that all situations are neutral. It's the label we put on them that makes them positive or negative. (I was a practicing Buddhist for a year, but I gave it up for my love of Scotch and adrenaline) Despite this, I learned that happiness is proven a choice.

To have everything you want in life all at the same time, you need to increase your ability to feel happy. Yes, increase your ability to experience joy and laughter on a daily basis. It's scientific. **You can increase your own capacity to feel happier.**

REPROGRAMMING YOUR HAPPINESS SET POINT

Psychologists refer to a 'happiness set point' that appears to largely determine our overall well-being. We flutter around this set point, becoming happier when something positive happens or vice versa, then returning to equilibrium or the 'happiness set point'. In some ways, we become sedentary in our expectation of happy feelings on any given day.

The exciting thing is that this set-point, to some extent, can be reprogrammed. The more happiness you experience in a day raises your brain's expectation of happiness. Your brain will adjust its expectation for on-going happiness. Your tolerance increases. You raise your daily average in a way. How do you do this? The best way is to find ways to laugh each day so that your brain interprets your laughter as additional moments of happiness. It changes your brain chemistry. By taking the time to find humor in everyday situations, you can reprogram your brain to expect a higher level of happiness.

CHOOSING LAUGHTER LEADS TO INSPIRED ACTION

During one of the most crucial times of my business recovery, my company survived a major natural disaster. A tornado hit the zip code where my building was located. Locked inside the building with dozens of employees we watched as trees flew down the road and electrical lines came crashing down. We watched in darkness. We listened with racing hearts. When the tornado passed, and I ventured outside to survey the scene, I realized that my 24/7 call center was not going to be up and running for weeks. The surrounding damage was massive. If my call center did not become functional within hours, we would lose money and clients: game over. There was a State of Emergency called both in New Jersey and at Synergixx.

My first response was "I can't believe this is happening to me. Why can't I catch a break?" Then as fast as I thought it, I retracted it. No one was hurt. My building had no damage. Now if I went out of business I would have a really good excuse – the Tornado did it!

I started laughing out loud, called Jenn and said: "Well, at least it wasn't another car crashing through the building." She was less amused during the call and accused me of being drunk because I was laughing about the tornado.

It was time for me to become the Unrealistic Saleswoman and sell myself on staying positive until the solution presented itself. I started selling myself:

'We only need electricity, folding chairs, and coffee to run a call center. Where does this all live in the middle of a tornado? How can I start a new call center in the next 60 minutes?'

The idea popped into my head. The thought was so crazy that I started laughing again. The next zip code over had power and a Marriott Hotel. That was my salvation I decided. Driving over to the hotel, avoiding fallen trees, power lines, parts of houses all in the middle of the street, I parked in the lot and went to the front desk at 9 pm.

"Hi! I'd like to rent three hotel rooms and all of your conference rooms twenty-four hours a day for the next week!"

"Ma'am, our general manager, would have to approve this, and he is not in until tomorrow at 9 am."

"Perfect! I will set-up in the conference rooms now and in the morning when he comes in, he'll know where to find me. Ready for a laugh?"

"Uh, ok."

"I'm about to start a call center in your hotel and my employees drink lots of coffee so room service will be super busy all week."

I walked away from the front desk and straight into the first conference room. I called members of my staff and with a grin on my face told them to bring every computer we owned to the Marriott and the telemarketers too. We had one hour to get back in business. This was going to be a fun adventure, I assured them. I even brought my kids to the hotel and had them help set-up our new call center. By the time the General Manager found us the next morning, we had taken more than 3000 calls in the makeshift, hotel conference room call center.

The amount of money it took to operate the business out of the Marriott was a crushing blow to our financial situation. It set us back. The uninterrupted service to our clients kept our business intact and would allow us to keep fighting our way to financial stability. I chose to be happy about that fact.

LOL GUYS ON SPEED-TEXT

A 2011 Michigan State University study found that workers who smiled as a result of cultivating positive thoughts exhibited improved mood and less withdrawal. Fake smiling, on the other hand, resulted in worse moods and withdrawal from work. So, when I get into a funk, I grab my cell phone and text a select group of friends. Almost 100% of the time I get back a text that makes me really laugh out loud. It's amazing what people can do with a whole 10 seconds to think.

> **MY TEXT: You have 10 seconds to make me smile. Make it funny cuz I need to laugh right now.**

FORCE HAPPINESS THROUGH SERVICE

Gandhi said it best. "The best way to find yourself is to lose yourself in the service of others" Helping other people forces you out of your mental funk and teaches you gratitude. Volunteer for things. Roll up your sleeves. Especially when all you want to do is stay in bed eating Pop Tarts (don't judge my guilty pleasures).

PRACTICE GRATITUDE

I don't count my blessings because I don't have enough fingers. Writing down the blessings in my life connects my thoughts to my body – the muscles in my hand speak to the muscles in my brain. On paper, I can see all the things I am taking for granted in my passing moments of unhappiness. Gratitude is an action, not a feeling. Once you have your list of blessings, reach out to the people on that list and tell them so. Drop them a sticky note at their desk with a thank you. Send them a note with a great picture on Facebook. Small gifts. A toast at the right moment. A call on a Tuesday night. Cook for them. There are many ways to show gratitude and it powers your happiness.

APPRECIATE YOUR PAIN

Sometimes life kicks you in the stomach. When you are doubled over, gasping for air, fighting back tears, remember that "this too shall pass." Once you can stand up, rather than hold on to the pain, ask yourself to search deep to find its meaning. Choose to look for the benefits that can be found in your trials. At the very least, perseverance is being built.

Life is a choice. It is YOUR life. Choose consciously, choose wisely, and choose honestly. **Laugh your ass off! Choose happiness – the alternative sucks.**

Chapter Four

Never Breast Feed Near the Water Meter!

A woman is like a tea bag—
you never know how strong she is until she gets in hot water.
—Eleanor Roosevelt

Birthing Babies: Corporate And Real

Serial entrepreneur and author Walt Sutton likens a new business to a baby. Care for it, nurture it, protect it, and it can be the most rewarding and fascinating experience of your life. Leave it alone for a minute and… well, let's not think about what could happen to it out there in the cruel world.

I'm willing to bet this guy Walt never tried to start a new business while breast feeding a ten-pound baby using a 44-inch feeding unit attached to his chest 24 hours a day!

Yes, becoming an entrepreneur can be a lot like having a baby. It's one of the most harrowing things you can do in life, and for some, the rewards make the risk and responsibility worthwhile. **Most anyone can start a business, just like most women can have a baby, but how well-prepared you are is often a crap shoot. In either scenario, you get to pick out a name.**

At this point, I had done both. My son, Jake, was four months old, and my company named Synergixx had just turned a month old. My office was the room off my living room, and it was fully equipped with a desk, computer, phone, fax and crib. Jake was an amazing baby who slept peacefully most of the time and cried only when he was hungry. I could get through large chunks of my business day with him quietly sleeping by my side.

Every morning I woke up and rushed down stairs to my home office and relished in the small things like checking my messages, creating a to-do list, and adding to my vision board. Even if I had not slept the night before because I was up with the baby, I still had the energy to run my business; I was in my power. I was in complete control of my life for once in my life. I was free!

It was in the initial few months of juggling the baby and the business that I thought, "Wow, this is easy. Why isn't every woman doing it?" And then as Synergixx turned two months old and Jake became a very alert five-month-old the answer to my foolish question became clear.

Jake was a happy baby born at almost ten pounds and by five months he was hungry *all* the time. When I wasn't breast feeding him directly, I was pumping and storing milk for later. I was a CEO alright – Chief of Engorgement Officer! Dairy cows had nothing on me.

I learned to type very fast with one hand while the other hand held either the pump or Jake himself. Tom bought me one of the new headsets that allowed both my hands to be free so I could carry on conference calls and change a diaper at the same time just by using the mute function.

When he could, Tom would strap Jake into a back-pack carrier and take him to school to lecture with him on his chest so I could work alone. On the days Tom couldn't help out, I planned my conference calls around Jake's naps as best I could. I didn't let any of my clients know I had a baby because I never wanted them to question my ability to handle their business. I never wanted the fact that I was a lady with a baby to be used as an excuse for not getting the job. But the longer I tried to hide the fact that I was nursing my baby during work hours the trickier it became. It was like the Universe was creating literal booby traps so I would get caught.

On one particular day, I had an important conference call with my client and a lawyer that was trying to shut down his TV infomercial – the first project I had done under the Synergixx name. If the commercial was taken off the air, I would lose the account. The client was very nervous. The attorney had limited time. I was out of my league. Tom couldn't be home, and we had no other options for child care at the time. Despite my best efforts to get Jake to sleep through the call, he woke up right at the beginning ready to eat a seven-course meal. This was not the call for my client to discover my secret; the attorney had already begun using choice language.

I quickly ripped open my blouse, buttons flying everywhere, and attached Jake to my body. In my panic, I had torn it in a way that left a large flap hanging down the side exposing my hideous nursing bra. My right arm cradled Jake and was pinned awkwardly to my side so I didn't even attempt to fix my blouse fearing that I would disturb Jake's trance-like sucking. I could already tell that my arm would fall asleep before the call ended. Hoping Jake would fall asleep while nursing I began to pace the room. The call continued for what seemed like forever, and I kept on pacing with my arm aching from holding Jake in place. My pacing began to pay off because I could see Jake starting to nod off. Just as I was preparing to put the headset on mute during another one of the lawyers tirades and remove Jake from my body, his head fell back in a milk coma. Immediately, my breast started squirting milk everywhere. I couldn't move my arm to cover up fast enough and due to the spewing milk from my right breast, my left breast decided to join in. I didn't want to wake him up and add to the chaos, so my actions were clumsy and slow. I desperately tried to cover up with my left hand completely forgetting I was not on mute. Jake was being sprinkled with milk as were the walls and my computer screen. Everywhere I turned there was milk. One breast is hanging out in the open squirting like a fire hydrant and the other hidden behind a dingy nursing bra creating a puddle inside the bra itself. Jake lay content in my arm asleep and smiling as if he knew what was happening.

As I reached up to mute the headset, I realized I was standing directly in from of the window facing the street. There was the water meter man on a routine check of my house's usage, staring open-mouthed at me and all the milk running down the window. I screamed from the shock, which completely panicked my client and the lawyer. The meter man turned and hurried to his car as I hung up and threw the headset across the room. Jake woke up startled and started howling which made my body spew even more milk. My arm was alive with painful pins and needles and my legs so wobbly I feared I would drop Jake. All I could think to do was drop down to the floor, below the curtain-less window, and lay Jake across my chest so his mouth would cover one of my squirting breasts while his diaper would plug up the leak on the other side.

When Tom finally arrived home, I was sitting on the floor against my desk smelling of spoiled milk with the headset on my lap and my five-month-old still sucking greedily. I was crying. He looked around at the window with dried, flaky milk residue. His eyes darted to the computer screen covered in a milky gray… his jaw dropped.

When he asked what had happened, I burst out into more tears and shouted "The meter man saw me naked and squirting milk on the windows. He ran away like he had just discovered he was a perverted pedophile of freakish mammals! He will probably turn off our water or raise our rates! My client has left four messages so far wanting to know if I was okay because I hung up the phone screaming. I can't call him back and tell him that the water meter man freaked me out while I was trying to control my udders from exploding! Working for myself was the wrong decision!"

He walked over and pulled Jake from my arms. He walked out to the kitchen and came back holding a bottle to Jake's mouth, and he continued to feed without a care in the world.

"Go take a bath and you'll feel better when you don't smell like cheese. I'll clean up your office as soon as he's done. If you still want to quit tomorrow, we'll start looking into day care centers, no sweat." As I let the hot water run over me, I thought about his words. Tomorrow we could call some daycare centers. That was not what I wanted. I vowed to keep my son home for the first year of his life. Many parents put their kids in daycare to work. I was raised by a nanny. There was nothing wrong with using a day care center so that I could run my business better – except we couldn't afford it.

No matter how I thought about it putting my son in a daycare center seemed like the most unnatural thing I could do. By the time I had dried my hair and walked downstairs Jake was happily asleep in Tom's arms. I sat down next to them, and we sat in silence for a while.

Tom broke the silence by saying out loud what I was thinking. "We need curtains in your office."

THEN WE NEEDED A NEW CARPET

Several months, later Tom left for three days for a conference in New Orleans while I was in the middle of a big project with a strict deadline. I would be alone with Jake to play the role of Single-Mom-CEO for 72 hours. No problem. I had planned my workload and conference calls around Jake's schedule.

And then life decided I had become too comfortable in my juggling act. Just as Tom's plane took off, my client called to tell me that the deadline was still firm, but some significant changes had to be made in the marketing piece. I assured him I would get it done. While Tom's plane was in the air, Jake started barfing. This was NOT just plain old ate-too-much, upset-tummy vomit – NO! This was full projectile vomiting with chunks. Kid vomit. No worries. Clean it up and keep him hydrated. No problem.

One of the misnomers of being the "boss of your own company" is that you control your schedule. Untrue. Your family and your clients control your schedule, especially in the early days. When you are the CEO, Creative Director, Client Services, New Business Person, CFO, and the Company's Fix-It person, there is never a good day to call out due to a sick kid – especially when most of the people you work with don't even know you have a child!

By the time Tom landed and called to check on us, Jake had vomited at least four times and was sleeping from exhaustion. I decided not to mention it to Tom so he wouldn't worry while he was away. Besides, hadn't I taken on the challenge of starting my own company so I would have the freedom to deal with all the challenges of mommy-hood?

That first day, I stayed up all night working on the clients' project stopping only to rock Jake back to sleep. I had slept for about two hours before I woke up to the lurching sound that was followed by the wet sound and then his cry. His crib was coated in milky, chunky, liquidly PUKE. I picked him and tried to settle him down, but his scared cries led to coughs that sparked more PUKE! On me. On the wall. On the floor. After an hour of this, I called his doctor who told me it was a stomach bug, "keep him hydrated" and it will pass.

As I hung up with the doctor, my office line began to ring. With the deadline approaching, vendors began calling with last minute questions. While I was talking to the vitamin manufacturer, Jake spewed all over my keyboard. While I was on a call with the printer, Jake let loose on living room carpet. If I tried to put him down just long enough to clean up the mess, he would cry until he coated his pack-and-play with bile. I refused to call Tom. What could he do but come home early? That wasn't fair to his career.

I would just work when Jake fell asleep. When he nodded off, I sent emails rather than make phones calls so I wouldn't get caught between a projectile episode and a client call. I worked on storyboards quietly while he slept so I could quickly get him to the bathroom should the moment arise. By the end of day two, I started prioritizing my activities: keep him hydrated, rock him to sleep, work on the project, send emails quickly, clean up the biggest mess and get to the little messes later. Repeat. Missing from my priorities was eating, sleeping, and showering. When Tom walked into the house on that third day, the stench knocked him back. The house was coated in dried vomit. I was lifeless on the couch holding Jake – both of us in dirty clothes and matted hair. The carpet between the front door and the living room couch was a minefield of wadded up bath towels and paper towels on top of vomit puddles. The air was thick with bile. My eyes were glassy.

"The doctor said he would be better in a few days. I thought I'd have this cleaned up before you got back. He hasn't stopped throwing up since you left but I think we are at the end of it," I mumbled.

"WOW! Why didn't you call me..." he was stunned and covering his nose, still one foot outside the house.

"I CAN handle it. He's fine now. I got the project out. Watch your step. It's everywhere." Tom slowly entered the house and took Jake out of my arms. The three of us went upstairs, and he bathed Jake as I showered. The last thing I remember him saying before I fell asleep naked, with a wet bath towel wrapped carelessly around me was, "We are definitely going to need a new rug."

Lesson Seven: Become a Parent Immediately

This lesson may be controversial for you, but I believe it wholeheartedly. There is no single endeavor more entrepreneurial than becoming a parent. Kids, at any age, teach you success lessons you can only learn in the process of parenting. It changes how you think and create. These lessons come in the form of emotions and experiences out of reach until you see yourself as a parent to a child. Become a parent as soon as possible.

Whether birthing a baby only appeals to you in business, or if all you can think about is one-day birthing a real baby, my advice is simple. Stop planning for it. Jump in both feet first – NOW!

As I said before, I believe all entrepreneurial women should become parents. I haven't met one mother (or father) who wouldn't die for their child. That's powerful. That's divine. Do you have someone you are willing to give it all up for... die for? I'm not talking about your significant other. It's not the same thing. Even if you think you don't want to have kids, can't have kids, think you're too busy for a kid, believe you wouldn't be a good parent, or think you can't afford to be a parent... that is not the question.

The question:
Do you have someone you are willing to die for?

Caring about someone else's safety, happiness, and success more than you do about your own is truly an experience no one should wait one minute longer to experience for the rest of their life. It is an amazing experience to care for someone or a group of someones' at this level.

Marriages, partnerships, friendships, and opportunities all come and go. Parenting – when it's great and when it is terrible – is something you do until your last breath. There is no time out when parenting.

There is no quitting. Imagine feeling that connected to something other than yourself – forever. In many ways, the desire to become a parent is a pretty selfish pursuit, if you really dig down deep.

There is no right way to become a parent. How you become a parent is a choice you get to make. You can go the stretch-mark route (with a spouse, lover, or with science) and pop a kid out from between your thighs, fully understanding that your hips will never go back to the same width as before. You can choose to adopt the child you never knew was meant for you but becomes your soul mate. Or you can be lucky enough to connect with a younger being that sees you as a parent and you accept them as your child. This child can be fostered, inherited, one that you see weekly or can even be a group of children. Their needs become your top priority. That's parenting.

Even if you never have children of your own, **I believe it is your responsibility as an entrepreneur to be a parent to someone in this world**. You will sacrifice for them before satisfying yourself. You will make sure that child succeeds, in part, as a direct result of your involvement in their life. You will integrate them into your life equally, making them part of your WHYs.

Being a parent is frightening, challenging, exhilarating, maddening, and joyful… it's addicting… it changes you. Keeps you humble. Grateful. Focused. Gives you drive and purpose when you might otherwise feel lost. It makes you prioritize your business and personal goals. It keeps a mirror in front of you. It keeps you from making decisions that keep you solitary in this world. Parenthood has a magical effect on your life. If you're already a parent, are you the best one you can be or is there room for improvement? If you haven't taken the plunge, there will never be a better time to put someone else first in your life. If you chose to read this book, there is a part of you that wants to be a parent but you are waiting for the right time. That time is now.

Chapter Five

Successfully Unbalanced

We cannot change what we are not aware of, and once we are aware, we cannot help but change.
—Sheryl Sandberg

My first year in business I earned three times the salary I did just one year prior working for someone else. I was positive that my sixteen hour days were paying off. I had made the right decision. Then one night Tom looked up and said, "I miss sex." The conversation started in my head.

I've been building a business while being used as a spit-up rag by our new son. I spend my days cooped up in my home office toggling between making sure the kid doesn't strangle himself on the fax line cord and talking to arrogant bastards who think it is so cute that my Daddy gave me a little boy's name. My hair is showing its roots for the first time in five years, and I catch myself wearing your underwear at least three times a week because I'm too busy to wash my clothes! All my clothes look like hand-me-downs that don't quite fit right because we couldn't afford

maternity clothes, and my new mommy-body has stretched everything in six different directions. I've been banking my sleep for months, hoping to use them for an eight-hour nap on my next birthday, while using so much concealer under my eyes that when I leave the house, I look like an albino raccoon. I haven't had anyone look at my TITS in more than a year without staring at me like I belong in a circus freak show. And just when I think the baby is down for the count and even attempt to sexy-up for an early evening of marital gymnastics, my phone rings and a client sucks the libido out of me with some demand that I need to fulfill. I do it because we need the paycheck, even though I know I'm being taken advantage of under the 'always give value-added' contract – the one you sign when starting your own business and become a slave to your clients! YOU miss sex! I miss being able to see my belly button in the same place God put it! Sex is how I got into this entire mess!

I chose to leave the room instead of trying to explain what I was feeling. As I stood in the shower, I realized I missed sex too! I missed many things about my pre-mommy life: stilettos, perfectly dyed hair, clothes that told people I was Tom's much younger wife, spontaneity, and the ability to drink a dirty martini on a whim without worrying about ruining the quality of my body's organic dairy farm production. Truthfully, I was too exhausted for sex because I had been so busy trying to prove to Tom and the world that I would win the Successful Mompreneur Medal of 2001. In that hot shower, it hit me that I had completely failed at being the wife I swore to be. Tom told me he understood that I had to spend so much time on the business and that he was proud of me for being the mother I was to Jake. He was sure that we would have our time when things settled down – I was riddled with guilt.

I had put us on an intimacy-free diet unintentionally. We were thinner now. Worse for the wear. Sex and passion are that important in an intimate relationship; I just didn't know how important at the time. I did admit I was no longer the exciting girl he had married. I was this tired, overworked, uncombed hair, sweat pant wearing shadow of myself. Hell, I wouldn't want to sleep with me.

How could I make more time for him and me when I barely had time for Jake and clients? The adrenaline of committing to two important life decisions at one time – mother and CEO – had fueled me straight through the sixteen hour days for twelve months. Now faced with the realization that I had to make time for my marriage – or give up something for my marriage – I was engulfed by guilt. I was a twenty-five-year-old first-time mom who was building a company in a world full of men without a mentor, a guide book, or safety net. I didn't think I had the luxury to stop running so fast because my mistakes would catch up to me and I'd fail. I started waking up in the middle of the night with the same question in my head.

Am I willing to screw up my marriage to be a successful entrepreneur?

I WAS SELFISH

The truth is this. I wasn't willing to give up anything. My husband was politely pointing out that my work life had severely impacted our marriage. I wasn't willing to give up the feeling of being the supermom who earned 3X times more than her previous boss had said she was worth. I wanted to be the mom, the CEO, and the wife all at the same time but was clueless when it came to balancing the three. I told myself that Tom and I would be okay. I told myself that once he saw how successful I became he would understand and forgive this period in our lives. I told myself that I deserved to be able to enjoy a growing business because I worked hard for it. I convinced myself that he should understand what I was going through and adjust. I was so wrong.

BECOMING INVISIBLE

It was our anniversary, and I had put on special lingerie for Tom. He was checking on Jake after paying the baby sitter that had afforded us a rare night out to dinner alone. I went into the bedroom and waited for him to follow and unwrap his gift. He would not miss sex tonight. I waited. And I waited, perfectly positioned on the bed for maximum impact of the lingerie. He never came. I put on a robe and went downstairs.

He was watching TV happily enjoying a Scotch. I stood in the doorway with my robe open just enough to reveal the lingerie I had picked out for this evening. He didn't look up. I moved and cleared my throat.

"Oh, hey! I thought you went to bed. Need something?" His eyes didn't leave the TV.

He wasn't mad. He was acting normal. Our new normal. My work schedule and my lack of attention had made me invisible to him as a lover. I was just his wife in a robe that perhaps needed some water before going back to bed. I was devastated.

Lesson Eight: Passion, Play, and Progress

As female entrepreneurs, we must take purposeful action to support every area of our life; Passion (personal desires), Play (family and community), and Progress (business). To be successful in everything, you must thrive in unbalance; happily applying some level of focus to each area of your life daily. Make being June Cleaver, Jessica Rabbit, and Drew Barrymore as much a priority as becoming Arianna Huffington, Amelia Earhart, and Oprah Winfrey. To do this, you must systematically build Passion, Play and Progress into your daily schedule.

It is not difficult to turn into the leader, inventor, business-woman, mother, wife, lover, friend and person you do not want to be. We chase this illusion of work/life balance; giving things up here and there to try and balance it all together. Then our lives get tangled and thin. It is a mirage. There is no balance – only purposeful actions.

That night of my anniversary, I realized I could lose my husband. Maybe he'd never leave me. Maybe he would. He had already stopped "seeing" me and my company hadn't even celebrated our second anniversary. What would happen when the company turned 3, 4, even 5 years old? It was a terrible feeling and it is a testament to Tom that my lust for building a business didn't permanently ruin the passion in our marriage. Not every man would be so patient. Relationships are fragile and sex is only one piece that holds it together. I woke up the next morning with a plan.

I decided every day I should work on each type of woman I wanted to make up my entire package. I was a mom, a wife, a CEO. But I also wanted to be a passionate woman, an artist, an author, a speaker, the best girlfriend, and so many other types of women. What I learned in the year and a half of trying to be all these types of woman at the same

time was that finding balance was an illusion. Some days required more of me as a mother while other days demanded almost 100% of my CEO brain. Days would go by when I would ignore entirely being a wife. So, I decided every day I would create specific plans to incorporate all these areas of my life into my activities. I would plan my 3Ps!

- **Passion:** It is important to wake up passionately every morning because without passion you are no good to the world. Passion comes in many forms and it is what drives all our senses, whether altruistic, entrepreneurial, artistic, or sensual. If you are not waking up feeling giddy and excited about your day, then something is wrong in your business, your relationship, your family, or all of the above. Success and passion are linked.

- **Play:** It is important to play each day; play keeps us energized, reduces stress, boosts creativity, and makes the arduous worth it. While playing may only take up 5 minutes or the majority of your day, you need to make sure you make time for it. As entrepreneurial women, we abandon play before all else when we are juggling things in life. This is one reason we become unfocused, discouraged, and drained. Playing is not selfish. It is a critical survival skill in the unbalanced life you will lead as an entrepreneur.

- **Progress:** Equally, it is important to feel like you've made specific progress in your life on a daily basis. The more days you go without identifying progress, the harder building your business and life becomes. The progress doesn't have to be major – just noticeable. If you don't plan your progress, you may not be able to recognize it. Progress is tangible.

Develop a routine of waking up every morning and taking the time to plan out how you will incorporate your 3P's into your day. This guarantees these important aspects of your life do not get lost in the chaos. The success secret here is thinking about them first thing every morning. It's a paradigm shift.

In the first five minutes I wake up, I am thinking about my 3 Ps. It's a habit, a meditation, and a life line. I create a list of activities that will engage my personal life, my family life, and my work life – no matter how hectic my day becomes. I need to make time for all the women I am inside.

PLAY: Play with your kids. Schedule play dates with your adult friends. Play with your pets. Go to the beach. Book a last minute get-away. Exercise. Play golf. Goof off. Dye your hair pink! Embrace your inner Peter Pan. Tell dirty jokes in line at the grocery store. Whatever makes you laugh – do it! If you want to be inspired, stress-free, and motivated to tackle everything all at once then you have to play every day even when all you want to do it cry and hide. I recommend thinking about how you will play each day BEFORE you think about anything else, so it doesn't get deprioritized.

PASSION: Passion. Passion. Passion. Find it. Engage in it. Share it. Be physical with it! It is any activity that gets your blood pumping and your toes curling, even for a short amount of time. Kiss longer than normal. Have sex- again! *(For me these two are usually the first things I think about – even though I recommend thinking about PLAY first. We can't help who we are!)* Passion can be found anywhere and anytime. Wear stilettos! Cook a meal that must be served on beautiful plates. Write something scandalous down on a napkin and leave it for the right someone to read. Paint on a real canvas. Make music. Jump out of a plane. Go on a blind date. Drink whiskey! Run a marathon. Flirt with the FedEx guy – daily if you can! Take up a hobby that you are terrible at, but that speaks to your soul. Engage in activities that frighten you and push you outside your comfort zone. Squealing is passion in verse! Have conversations that push your buttons with people you admire. If you don't feel excited every day when getting out of bed, you need a bigger Passion List!

PROGRESS: Let's face it! Progress in our business and personal life makes Play and Passion easier and more enjoyable. Before you get out of bed in the morning, decide on at least one thing you can do that day to create progress in your business and personal life. Make a hard phone call to an unprofitable client. Fire an employee. Hire a new employee. Meet with your accountant. Raise your rates. Place an ad on LinkedIn. Create an employee handbook. Finish the project on deadline. Get to the gym for only 15 minutes. Say sorry to your lover for your part of the argument. Schedule the breast exam. Join the Mastermind webinar for a half-hour. There is no progress too small or too big as long as you are making it daily. Get these tasks done as early as possible in the day to help relieve stress, set the tone for the day, and to clear your mind.

Life is too short, business changes too quick, and love dies suddenly. You cannot afford to wait to start any part of your life. You need to act and react to emerging opportunity. There will never be a perfect time to start your business. Investing doesn't get less risky. There is never a better time to become a parent. And falling out of love is easier than falling in love. You need to live your life all at the same time and fight for what is important.

- Do you want to be the woman who spends years building her career and then decides she wants a meaningful personal relationship?
- Do you want to be the woman who spends years raising a family before she takes time to focus on your career options?
- Do you want to wake up one day and realize you've waited too long to have a family, even though you have a great career and partner?
- Or are you willing to risk feeling regret for choosing one over the other entirely?

You can have it all at the same time – and should. The clock is ticking! Don't try and live a balanced life by cutting out activities because you feel there is no time in your day. Make the time to nurture every type of woman you want to become. Get comfortable with being successfully unbalanced.

When it comes to having it all at the same time, people will tell you compromise is involved. To have massive financial success, you will need to miss a few recitals – I say that's crap! To grow your business, you will have to work so hard that your marriage or relationships may suffer for a little while – I say that's more crap! To have a business and a family, you have to sacrifice friendships or personal growth – you know exactly what I am going to say… CRAP times infinity! Just plan your 3P's and get creative in how you fit them into your day. For example:

- Get a pedicure while on a conference call.
- Watch your favorite movie while folding laundry and baking cookies.
- Hire a housekeeper to free up two extra hours in your life.
- Have a business meeting while pushing the stroller and getting your walk in for the day.
- Hire a driver to take you on trips longer than an hour so you can work while they fight traffic.
- Have sex as soon as you wake-up and shower at the gym.
- Trade a Monday at Disneyland with the kids for a Saturday at the office.

You are a smart and determined woman. Find ways to combine your activities so you can make time for everything. Make your day a game. Some days you will be more successful than others at executing the 3Ps. The success secret here is thinking about them first thing every morning and learning how to juggle your time better.

Chapter Six

Electrical Sockets, Prostitutes, & Friday the 13th

Don't be intimidated by what you don't know. That can be your greatest strength and ensure you do things differently from everyone else.

—Sarah Blakely, inventor of SPANX

THE QUICK START ENTREPRENEUR

"Girls have an unfair advantage over men: if they can't get what they want by being smart, they can get it by being dumb."

I read this quote on the back of a barroom napkin. It comes from Rodgers & Hammerstein's musical *The King and I* where Yul Brynner says this line about his co-star Deborah Kerr. When I first read it, I was appropriately offended, especially since it was a cocktail napkin in a no-name bar. I kept the cocktail napkin for many years, planning to pull it out at party one night to stimulate conversation. One Saturday I rediscovered the crinkled napkin, and when I read the quote again, it made sense to me. Timing is everything when developing clarity.

Let's fast forward through year two and three. Here are the highlights.

My first year I produced six TV infomercials and four radio shows for companies that called me days after discovering I had left the firm in Maine. The shows were a success and business was steady. I managed to save enough money by the end of the year to hire my first employee. I recruited a girl my age, Jenn, whom I had worked with in Maine. With a good sales pitch and the promise of a sign on bonus in the form of a DVD player I convinced her to leave everything she knew and move to South Jersey to help me expand the business. Jake was starting preschool, so there was plenty of room for her desk in my home office – goodbye pack-n-play! I would be able to take on double the work load, and she would help me service the clients so we could expand. Simple. We spent most of this year actively securing new business. We packed overnight bags and flew to conventions to solicit new business. We were a dynamic duo with fantastic high heels.

Then we received a huge break. A large retail client, run by a very aggressive entrepreneur, was referred to Synergixx. This man met with us for two hours and signed on the dotted line. He hired Synergixx not only to produce eight half-hour radio shows but also his print catalog (no internet to speak of at the time). He also wanted us to buy his media and train his call center operators. He knew I had experience in these areas and even though Synergixx was only a production company at the time, he thought we should handle the media as it was easier for him to use a one-stop-shop.

We were so excited that we never considered if we could pull it off with just the two of us, very limited operating capital, and no systems in place to manage media. But we said yes and off we went. Two months later, with $50,000 in our bank account, we sat on the back porch of my house getting drunk off Dirty Martinis. We were not celebrating.

Synergixx had risen to the challenge; produced eight shows, successfully purchased media, and designed a stellar print catalog. I had personally trained the client's call center in Florida. Everything was set for success. Except that the very aggressive entrepreneur had asked us to schedule 100% of his media over one weekend so he could quickly know if he had winners. The problem was that his call center in Florida did not stay open all weekend and hadn't told anyone this fact. Monday morning we discovered that the call center had abandoned more than 50% of the calls generated by the radio shows we had produced. The client knew this was not Synergixx's fault, yet his entire test budget had gone into the weekend media and without the corresponding phones sales, he was forced to shelve the project entirely.

Synergixx had the money for a production job well done, but we had lost the client and the continuing revenue it would have brought to the company. We had also dedicated almost 100% of our time to working with this flagship client over the past four months that our pipeline was empty with no new business lined up. We only had fifty thousand dollars in the bank to cover expenses and salaries for the rest of the year. We were now vulnerable again.

Here is where the *"King and I"* quote comes in. Sitting on the porch, martini in hand, I made a passionate declaration.

"If we had owned that call center this would have never happened. We should open a call center and then we can protect our clients and grow their business without anything getting in the way. We will become a One-Stop-Shop for our clients for real."

YUP! Drunk on my back porch, I made the decision to open a call center. It was the dumbest idea I ever had that paid off.

Less than thirty days later, the two of us were on our knees plugging phones into the wall of an old deli, high heels facing up to the ceiling, with only hours left before we took our first phone call in the new Synergixx Call Center. We had managed to find a phone service provider that would extend us 30-day terms and they drop-shipped the phone system to us directly. We had figured out how to make the system work, which was a huge win since neither Jenn nor I had any experience in IT or phone systems. We had twenty phones all connected to a server that allowed us to answer calls for multiple clients and tracked the calls for billing. We also had various cords that were too short or too long for the 8-foot folding tables we had set up as desks. We had duct tape holding down wires. We caused several of the electrical sockets to spark when we plugged in too many extension cords. Folding tables for a desk.

Pads of paper for taking orders. Cups full of pens. A Mr. Coffee on a small college refrigerator for a breakroom. We were a skin-and-bones call center. Dressed up in our cutest business suits, the two of us stood in the middle of that old deli, the only decoration a black and white poster of Alexander Graham Bell talking on the telephone.

We looked very much in charge, but we were praying inside. Praying that we had hooked up the phones correctly. Praying that we had programmed the server correctly. Praying that the company who agreed to be our first call center client with a TV infomercial we had produced would generate the calls we anticipated starting at 2 pm. Praying that the ten employees we had hired from the local college would answer the phones and sell. Praying that the fifteen thousand left in our bank account would carry us through until the new revenue from the call center kicked-in.

Within four months of the call center being open, we had 50 employees answering five thousand calls a week, and we were growing every week. I had also just signed our largest production deal to date: 35 TV infomercials to be completed interview style within sixty days with all the calls coming to our call center. We were off to the races. From the 35 TV infomercials we produced, seven worked very well with one becoming one of the top infomercials of all time: Dual Action Cleanse.

Dual Action Cleanse took Synergixx from "a cute idea that girl Charlie had" to a nationwide success that employed thousands of people across the industry; call centers, fulfillment houses, manufacturing companies, and media companies. It grossed millions the first year and played on every TV station possible. It was my first serious hit since leaving my previous company. So we splurged on cubicles and chairs with padding!

DID I MENTION I WAS PREGNANT – AGAIN?

The call center was booming even though we were still taking phone orders on paper because we couldn't afford computers. Production jobs kept rolling in which meant I was in the production studio in Philadelphia most days. Jenn was left to run the budding call center in New Jersey. We were making it up as we went along.

"What possessed you to get pregnant now?" Jenn was in disbelief. "No worries. I'm good at being pregnant. It won't get in the way." Jenn became the back bone of the call center and ran all the operations including hiring, firing, IT issues, payroll, building issues, and anything that went wrong. I would come into the call center after a day of editing feeling creatively free and see Jenn running around with three heads.

On one particular day, Jenn looked like she could use a break. So I decided to make her a cup of tea. I grabbed a mug from the break room and put it in the microwave. Meanwhile, I walked out onto the sales floor where she was using her high heel to hold down a cable while she wrapped a label around one end that read: phone 51. Cool! We had added another phone to the sales floor – business must be good!

"Charlie, we are getting too many calls. You need to slow things down. We can't handle the growth. I have reps working 24 hours a day and four data entry people working full time just to keep up with the paper orders. Without computers, we are getting farther behind the more calls we take. You are going to have a baby soon and be here even less and I have to deal with this growth myself. Can't you tell clients to send us fewer calls while we get up to speed better?"

"Jenn, don't worry. This is only temporary. We will add computers in a few months. Besides, our reps are beating out all the other call centers so maybe computers actually make people sell less. It will be fine." Then the fire alarm went off.

We looked back into the break room where black smoke was billowing out. Immediately, the two of us ran into the smoke-filled room and saw that the microwave had a fire inside it. Jenn opened up the door, and more smoke blew out revealing a flaming cup.

"You put a travel mug in the microwave! It's metal!" She was frantic and outraged at my stupidity at the same time.

"It's my pregnancy brain!" And without thinking I reached into the microwave with crumpled up newspaper and grabbed hold of the flaming travel mug. Jenn opened the back door of the building, and together, the two of us escorted the coffee cup out of the back door. By the time we got outside the newspaper had also gone ablaze, so I flung the coffee cup out into the dirt parking lot.

"Are you crazy? Now we are going to catch the back of the building on fire too!" Jenn ran back inside and came back with a two-liter bottle of Coke, pouring it over the flames.

"I can't believe you did that Charlie!"

"What was I supposed to do? Call the fire department for blowing up a travel mug?"

"If you tell Tom that I let you touch a flaming coffee cup while pregnant, I will quit. Tom will kill me if he finds out. Damn it. How can I keep up this growth IF YOU ARE AN IDIOT?"

In the middle of our argument, we both realized the fire alarm was still blaring. Running back into the building, we were surprised to notice none of the phone reps had gotten off the phones and were still talking to customers despite the room filling with smoke. We assured people things were safe and began opening all the doors to get the smoke out. Later when I asked a sales rep why they hadn't gotten out of the building when the alarm went off, they answered, "We figured you two had it under control."

WET T-SHIRT CONTEST

We had it under control alright. So much under control that one night, when I randomly decided to go back to the call center and work late, I found only two employees in the building instead of the ten that were scheduled.

"Where is everyone? Where's the Shift Leader?"

I was politely informed that the local bar was hosting a wet t-shirt contest and that one of our employees had entered. The Shift Leader, along with the others on the shift, opted to take a long lunch break to show their support.

NEGOTIATING WITH COPS

Under control? We were trying to control growing pains for sure. Several times the police would arrive at the building asking for an employee that had a warrant out for their arrest. Nothing deadly – more like dead-beat parents that owed child support or missing court appearances. The police were coming to arrest them. The police seemed to time their arrival with the TV stations playing our infomercials because as soon as they knocked on the call center door, the phones would light up, and we would start selling. The calls were pouring in and piling up waiting for a sales rep to answer. We were understaffed. "Officer, I completely understand you have to take my guy into custody. All I am asking is that you wait fifteen minutes while he helps me clear the queue of calls. We pay good commission, and this would help him get square with his child support, right? Just come back in fifteen minutes and I'll send him right out." And when that didn't work? "How much to post bail? I really need them on the phones this weekend." That first year we controlled our growth by posting bail for more than a few non-violent offenders that had a gift for selling TV infomercial products.

MAKING MONEY IN THE BATHROOM

It continued to get out of control. We couldn't have dreamed up the human resource issues we would encounter. With fifty plus employees, in under nine months, working all shifts, we were stacking the deck against ourselves without even realizing it. I remember walking into the call center one afternoon after a long editing session in the city and watching Jenn cross the 3500 square foot call center in four long steps. "I NEVER signed up to be the BLOW JOB COP! There is a girl in my office trying to convince me that what she does on her break time is none of my business AFTER I caught her on her knees, with another rep, in the same bathroom I use. And Charlie Fusco if you dare ask me if she's a 'CLOSER' so help me God I'll quit right now!"

I HIRE MY DAD WHO HIRES PROSTITUTES

With no business plan, explosive growth, the fraternity-like distractions, fires, cops, and sexual mishaps, the only sound thing to do was to hire my retired, eccentric father to become my human resources manager. And that's exactly what I did.

"Charlie, this may be a sore subject, but I'm pretty sure your father just hired a troupe of prostitutes to be sales agents as a second job. Real prostitutes." Jenn had the 'how did we get here' look on her face.

When I confronted my father about his new hires, he was appalled, shocked, disappointed... he reduced me to a four-year-old version of myself.

"Charlie, I didn't raise you to judge others. These ladies have obvious sales skills, and if they have an alternative to their night time activities, then we should help them take it."

There was no convincing him that this type of second-job person did not reflect our corporate vision. The ladies he hired all had set times they could work and were very open with their dialogue in the call center. Were they the best choice? The answer didn't matter. The father-daughter relationship had changed the day he started. He was in charge of personnel, and I was in charge of getting more clients. He wouldn't discuss it. He saw a higher purpose in teaching these prostitutes how to get out of the pleasure career by giving 'good phone' and generating sales for colon cleansing products. The call center was evenly divided between college kids who all sat on the left side and the very experienced ladies who all sat on the right; my father walked down the middle.

MY WATER BREAKS ON FRIDAY THE 13TH

Let it go on record that I started Synergixx to be a TV producer, not an HR director. I seldom fired people. It just wasn't comfortable doing it because it seemed mean. However, on this particular day, I was attempting to fire an employee. After a half hour of talking with him, I got the feeling he wasn't getting the point that he could no longer collect a paycheck with Synergixx. Then it happened. My water broke as I'm sitting directly across from him, making a big puddle on the floor that spread to touch the edges of his Nike sneakers.

"Oh my God!" he whispered.

"Oh, sorry about that," I remained exceptionally calm as I was focused on trying to fire him. "So listen, I have limited time. I need to know if you understand that we can't continue your employment."

"Do you need me to call 911? Can I get you something? I can drive you to the hospital. Can you breathe?" His eyes locked in on my stretch-pant-covered vagina. He was having a conversation with my crotch. He couldn't hear my mouth saying, 'You're Fired' because he was too busy looking at the soaked area between my thighs expecting IT to answer back!

"I need you to tell me you understand that you don't work here anymore. Then I can drive myself to the hospital, okay."

"Right. I'm fired. But perhaps I should work here until you have the baby. It could take a really long time."

It was Friday the 13th. I chalked up the awkward conversation to a disruption in the universe, not my poor management skills.

I didn't end up driving myself to the hospital since Jenn, observing the whole situation, had called Tom who was on his way. I went from firing this employee to a car and into labor in about twenty minutes total in the middle of a major thunder and lightning storm. The hospital was running on generators, and the nurses were discombobulated having to revert to paper charts instead of entering information directly into the computer. I focused on not delivering a baby on Friday the 13th, so I refused any of their efforts to "speed up the delivery" which they wanted to do given the storm and chaos of the hospital. People have called me stubborn. That night I stubbornly commanded my body to hold it together until Ava Rose was born just after midnight on the 14th. Ava was born on a Saturday and by Monday, she was sleeping next to my desk in my home office. Business as usual.

I am positive that in the early days, we were being watched by a higher power. Watched by angels with a sense of humor. They looked down from up there, making sure we didn't kill ourselves but laughing the whole time as we bumbled our way through a monumentally poorly planned idea.

Looking back at the what, the how, and the why of opening a call center within eighteen months of starting a new business with no financial backing, no business plan, and no experience – what was I thinking? It was a plain dumb and unrealistic endeavor.

Yul Brenner wasn't saying that Deborah Kerr was more or less intelligent than a man. At least that's not the way I chose to view it. He was simply speaking to the fact that a passionate woman makes decisions that often seem unrealistic. It is the appearance of the unrealistic decision that to the outside world and even to herself that seems dumb - only because the passionate idea needs to be brought into reality.

FEAR OF FAILURE HIDDEN BY EGO

I had been successful despite my lack of planning because of my reputation, my creative talent, and my ego. I allowed my ego to be fueled by my success. My head was so big. I was making decisions that were not linked to my Core Drivers: about the types of employees we were hiring, about how poorly I treated my father as an employee, about how I looked the other way when I knew I was pushing my team too hard, and about how easy I was making my life seem to the outside world. I felt guilty every time I made a decision. I didn't ask anyone's opinion or advice on how my business was progressing.

What I was able to realize years later was that I had started my business with 100lb bag of resentment. I carried around this bag every day and the weight of it caused me to take liberties that were just plain dumb. I resented working my butt off in high school to get into a great University only to have my scholarship 'taken away'. I resented the jobs I was 'forced' to take just to get by. I resented my friends who got to experience the young college years without 'burdens' like mine. I resented the almost four years of hard work I had put into the company in Maine only to be told that 'a promotion was premature.' I resented being a woman who had to 'make herself smaller' in the man's office just to make him more money. I resented. So my early success became my 'stick it in your ear'. Look at me go! Catch me if you can! Except every day I experienced another success, I was convinced THEY would discover that I was a fraud.

Chapter Seven

Conquering Your F-Words

Don't compromise yourself. You are all you've got. There is no
yesterday, no tomorrow, it's all the same day.
—*Janis Joplin, legendary singer/songwriter*

BUSINESS AS USUAL

Going into year four business was gang busters. Jenn and I had
settled into running a company with a large staff and payroll. The bank
had given us a capital line of credit that allowed us to computerize our
call center. We had successful campaigns on TV and radio that were
generating the calls we needed to keep profitable. It was six-day work
weeks. We doubled our gross revenue for production, media and call
center, now topping five million a year. I was living every entrepreneur's
dream.

Ava was about eight months old and came to the office with me
every day. I was juggling Motherhood and CEOhood effortlessly. I made
every business meeting and every school event for Jake. I'd even figured
out how to have enough time alone with Tom, so our relationship was
stronger than ever. My bold decisions were paying off.

My children were happy, and my husband had nothing to complain about – I had figured out how to balance the nursery, the office, and the bedroom – FINALLY!

We Interrupt Your Regularly Scheduled Program

What kind of mother decides to die and get married in the same 48 hours? You read this correctly; die and get married in the same 48 hours. My mother.

There is a separate book to be written called *"I Got My Mothers Feet,"* which details the true story of the relationship I had with my mother and why despite all the not-so-great-stuff we went through I credit her almost 100% for my entrepreneurial drive. The bizarre details of our story together are saved for that book. For this one, here is what you need to know…

It was a Thursday, and I was in the office of one of the largest film and video companies in Philadelphia. I had brought them so much business in the last few years that the owner was offering me free office space in their prestigious high-rise building in the center of Philadelphia. Along with the office space, he would allow me to use any of his staff (directors, lighting team, editors, and set designers) to sit in meetings under the Synergixx name when I was pitching clients. I could even use their fancy boardroom. In exchange, I was to announce to the industry that his company and mine had formed a strategic partnership. He was willing to let me do all this with no investment up front; only a guarantee of all my production business going forth.

"Charlie, you're doing really well bringing in production jobs. Imagine if you had an office that looked like mine and an incredible, award-winning staff at your disposal. Clients will feel more confident in your ability. Your young girl company will get to big girl status overnight. You're doing well now. With the prestige of my company backing you, imagine how much better it could be?" Before I could digest what he was saying, my Blackberry rang.

"Charlie, the hospital released your mother. She is at my house. She is going to be there until it's over. The doctors say she won't last forty-eight hours. You need to come home no matter what." My Aunt Rose was always good at being blunt, and I was very good at showing no emotion in a business meeting.

"I really appreciate your generous offer. It's a lot to take in. Can you give me a few days to think about it?" My young girl company was grossing more than seven million dollars. I wondered how much I should have grossed to be considered a big girl company in his eyes. Would this alliance with him be the answer?

With no time to think, I booked five tickets to California on my American Express. We landed hours later with overnight bags. The first and last time my mother had met Tom she had looked past him and told me that he would "give me two-headed babies," referring to his profession in the theater that she assumed was fueled by experimental drug use. This was only one of the many stereotypes my mother knew to be fact in her mind. My father came with us out of respect for the family. He was stubborn because after ten years of court battles, he and my mother were still not divorced and he was holding a grudge. Jake asked why he never knew he had another grandmother besides 'Daddy's mommy.' The whole situation was awkward and stressful.

To remain focused, I checked my Blackberry every five minutes trying to manage my company remotely, keeping in the back of my mind that I had three important pitches the following week and wondered if they would go better in the fancy boardroom.

My Aunt Rose's house turned into a hostel for a mini family reunion with aunts, uncles, and cousins arriving to pay their last respects. I was surprised to discover my mother had a boyfriend who was also there greeting the family. It didn't take long before he and my father were on the back porch having a beer. The mood was somber, but my family was excited to meet the family of my mother's long lost daughter.

I walked into the room where she was to spend her final hours. It smelled like chemicals. She lay on the bed surrounded by pill bottles. Jake and Ava met the grandmother I never spoke about in this dimly lit room. She smiled, barely able to turn her head or lift up her hands. Jake gave her a kiss and then ran off looking for his aunt and a snack. Tom took Ava from me. I was alone with my mother for the first time in ten years. "Thank you for bringing my grandchildren to see me. They are beautiful. You are a good mother, I can see."

We exchanged small talk for a bit and then when it became too much for me to avoid a moment longer, I asked her a question.

"Do you have any regrets?"

She thought for a moment and said, "I never had a white wedding. I should have done a white wedding with one of my husbands."

What the FUCK? On her death bed, with hours to live, facing her estranged daughter for the first time in a decade, and her only FUCKING regret is NOT HAVING A WHITE WEDDING? What about me?

I was looking for an apology. I was outraged. I was pissed. I deserved an apology. I had no words for her. She was lying there, not even 60-years old, a yellowish-green from a failing liver after years of too much alcohol, with matted hair, and she smelled like a Mr. Clean bottle – and all she regretted was not having a white wedding?

I flew to be by her side within hours of getting the call, dragging my entire family along and listened to my father complain the entire way that he wanted a divorce before she died. All she could do was muse about how she could have had a white wedding with her current boyfriend but time had run out. This woman, my mother, had balls! These were balls the size of Texas. No! Antarctica balls – big, cold as ice, polar bear balls!

"Fine. Fine. Fine. Will your boyfriend agree to marry you? I'll have you married in white by the end of tomorrow, ok? YOU just don't die before two o'clock because I don't want to waste my time looking for a white dress for nothing." I was intentionally mean. She smiled and despite her yellow-green skin and puffy body she looked radiant. It pissed me off. Her death bed radiance. I was angry. I wanted an apology. She was making me feel like a child throwing a tantrum.

I spent the entire night on my Blackberry engrossed in running my business. I think I answered every email twice. I called Jenn hourly to make sure things were handled. I called clients for no reason. I even signed up for a conference in New York the following month.

As soon as the stores opened, I dragged my Aunt Rose all over town. We bought wedding rings from K-Mart; oversized white nightgowns from JC Penney, small bride and groom figurines from the Party Store, food for the reception from Rosie's Bar and Grill, as well as flowers for both the wedding and the funeral from Conrad's Florist on the corner of Reseda Blvd. My aunt and I were equal partners in crime for this illegal dying-wedding.

"Father, I would like to make a donation to your Parish. Also, I would like to ask you to fulfill a request for my dying mother."

"Of course my child. How may I help?" He was sweet and warm. "I need you to marry her by 2 pm today. To her boyfriend. She only has a few hours to live and wants to be married in white. Would you be able to marry her and read last rites at the same time given the circumstances?" I was trying to be professional standing on the steps of a beautiful Irish Catholic Church. He stared back at me trying to process it all. It occurred to me that withholding details from a man of God was not a good idea.

"I understand this is not customary. In full disclosure, my mother refuses to completely divorce my father, and he will be attending the wedding. I'm pretty sure she just enjoys antagonizing him year after year. Or maybe she doesn't like the idea of having two divorces under her belt. Or she thinks he is hoarding some money somewhere, and if she holds out long enough he'll have to split it with her. It could be because he hasn't asked her for a divorce in the right tone. Doesn't matter. She is Catholic, and she could be staying married because she promised God. Also, I'm not entirely sure her boyfriend has a Green card yet. But he has to be a nice guy because he agreed to marry a dead woman in a dress from JC Penney. That counts as a form of marital love, I think. And if I am completely honest the fact that you are an Irishman may not sit well with my mother. But she wants a white wedding. She won't make it through the night. Two o'clock? Yes?"

"This is… not very… typical… I…" he was trying to represent God in his best capacity. Perhaps withholding details was a better strategy.

"I completely agree. Again, I would like to make a donation to your Parish. Do you accept checks?" I was always selling something.

With her cremation and church service paid and set for the following week, my dying-wedding checklist was complete. I had managed to answer all my emails too. By two o'clock, in the backyard of my Aunt Rose's house, with twenty people in attendance, my mother sat in a chair at the make-shift alter and had her white wedding. Her unrealistic vision was turning into a reality right before my eyes.

Then she did it again. She altered reality. She refused to die for several more weeks. Refused! The doctors couldn't understand it because her liver and heart were hours away from shutting down when they sent her home. How could she have lasted several more weeks? My aunt said that it was typical from my mother.

"Even growing up, she always stayed longer at the parties where she felt everyone was looking at her." It would be years before I would understand my mother's death. More importantly, I had no idea that I would need to call upon this parting lesson my mother taught me at the most critical time.

BUSINESS AS UNUSUAL

I was advised to take some time off, but I was all about business as usual. I had my feelings tucked neatly into a box in my mind so I could focus completely on being a CEO and a Mom to my own children. When I arrived back at the office, no one could tell I had lost my mother.

A week after her death, I took a very tough lunch meeting with a big client, in which he was building a very strong case for why he should not have to pay his final bill in full. He had preplanned to have the conversation in a public restaurant with others at the table. I was completely taken off guard. I felt shocked, embarrassed, unsure, angry, afraid, helpless, responsible, and rejected all at once. Why do men like to have these type of conversations surrounded in garlicky foods?

As he aggressively laid out his argument in front of his other employees, his wife, and one of my key employees – politely, calmly, and with definitiveness. I sat quietly, trying not to show any emotion on my face. He was wrong. But how could I tell him that and save the relationship for future business? How could I tell him I couldn't afford the $20K deduction?

FEARING FAILURE MORE THAN BELIEVING IN SUCCESS

What I should have done was tell him exactly how I felt in plain, non-emotional language. He was blaming the poor execution on his end on my work and expected me to foot the bill. I should have pointed out all the facts that supported how well my company had handled his projected, gone above and beyond, and why his losses were not my responsibility. I should have stuck up for myself. But what if I lost him as a client? What if I wasn't as good as I thought I was?

He ended his diatribe by requesting a 50% reduction in the bill, and I excused myself to the restroom. I barely made it into the stall before the tears fell. The kind of tears accompanied by heavy breathing but no real sound. I was trembling. I was frantic because I couldn't stop the tears. I tried to keep my face from getting red and my mascara from running. I was conscious of the time I was in the bathroom – what would the people at the table think about why I was taking so long? I was mad at myself for reacting this way. I thought, 'this is what it feels like when you realize you really can't compete with the big boys.'

The lunch meeting ended with me going back to the table, agreeing to his request, and then trying not to let my jaw hit the floor when he said, "I knew you would be flexible. Let's get dessert and celebrate a great partnership!" I agreed. I agreed. I agreed. I agreed! I AM A FUCKING LOSER! Or whatever is worse than that…

I have done many things I am not proud of, yet none come so close to the top of the list as the way I handled myself during this meeting. For years later, I felt like a fraud. I was afraid of what might happen if I said enough is enough. This constant fear of being found out and potential failure followed me in business and personally.

99

Lesson Nine: Conquering Your F Words

Female entrepreneurs must overcome self-imposed feelings of fraud, fear, failure, and know that sometimes the only appropriate thing to say is *Fuck it!* or *Fuck off!* or *Fuck you*!

There is no polite way to say this. So make sure no one is around you when you say it out loud. And you should do it very loud, so you hear yourself! Say it with me! "Fuck fearing I'm a fraudulent failure!" Feels kind of good, doesn't it?

Conquering your 'F-Words' helps you determine how to use these words in your life to be successful faster and with less stress.

Tina Fey, an admirable comedian, has said, "The beauty of the impostor syndrome is you vacillate between extreme egomania and a complete feeling of: 'I'm a fraud! Oh God, they're on to me! I'm a fraud!' So you just try to ride the egomania when it comes and enjoy it, and then slide through the idea of fraud."

Kate Winslett, the star of my guilty-pleasure movie Titanic, was quoted as saying "Sometimes I wake up in the morning before going off to a shoot, and I think, I can't do this. I'm a fraud."

Here is the big one! Maya Angelou, who inspires entire nations with her poetry, admitted "I have written eleven books, but each time I think, 'Uh-oh, they're going to find out now. I've run a game on everybody, and they're going to find me out."

The crazy phenomenon I am speaking about is contagious. Emma Watson (actress), Sheryl Sandberg (Chief Operating Officer of Facebook), and Sonia Sotomayor (Associate Justice of the Supreme Court) were infected too! All have admitted to feeling like they'd be found out as frauds.

Ladies, if you desire the life of an entrepreneur, you'd better make sure you have the ego for it. Our egos do help us hang in during the 'fraud, fear, failure period' we all seem to go through. This period is like entrepreneurial puberty where everything gets you excited, but everything also feels like it is pointing in the wrong direction. Ego is a good thing to have on this road because it keeps you moving forward while you figure out how to use those F words.

Conquering The Fear Of Failure And Feeling Like A Fraud

Fear of failure is a self-sabotaging behavior. The overwhelming sentiment growing inside of us, gnawing at us, and saying, "You can't do this," is what deters us from our goal. Once we shift our mindset from being the victim to being our own salvation, we can turn 'screw-ups' into 'fail-ups'. Just accept that you will screw-up (make the wrong Activating Decisions). Failing is just a 'do-over' that allows you to move upward in your pursuit. Just proceed with the belief that you can handle things not working out, and you can create a new solution when it doesn't work out.

When you accept the risk of failure, with the belief that you will learn from it, then failure becomes only the number of attempts before you finally succeed.

So start doing more things that you're scared of screwing up! Go on one more blind date. Go to the bank and ask for the loan to start your new company. You can only stop being afraid of failure once you have lived through it a few times. I wasted so much time worrying about failing. What if I lost business, employees, friendships, and opportunities? Guess what? Even at my most cautious of moments those things happened. I had a bad habit of not firing bad employees because I thought I needed them to get by. Then, while I was agonizing over how to replace them, they quit and left me in a lurch. Had I fired them when they should have been let go, I would be in the same position except by my design.

Here's another reason I think women fear they will fail. We love pedigrees. We rate ourselves on everything. Look at me. Growing up, I thought that a prestige education would be my salvation. While I was still in high school, I was taking classes at Northwestern University.

Then I got accepted to Boston University and took 21 credits a semester only to finish up at the University of Southern Maine. As a result of my screw-ups I had to work 5X more than I studied just to pay for my prestigious education – all while dancing in a cage. Do you think I have a pedigree that makes me better than anyone else? I barely remember who was President of the United States during those years. It was all a blur.

Maybe you don't have a degree, or you think you need extra training in a field to get started, and that's why you feel like a fraud in certain circles. Give it up! **You have the intelligence to learn anything you need to succeed when you are ready.**

Don't worry about credentials! **Coco Chanel**, founder of the fashion brand Chanel, is iconic and has no degree. **Debbi Fields**, founder of Mrs. Fields Cookies, **Joyce C. Hall** founder of Hallmark, **Mary Kay Ash** founder Mary Kay Inc., and **Rachael Ray**. Celebrity Chef – all these women have no 'pedigree.' Even in the tech industry you can find proof that pedigree is not everything. **Jeri Ellsworth** is a college drop-out and a self-taught engineer credited with squeezing 8-bit home computer Commodore 64 onto a single chip and tucked into a joystick that connects to a television set via cable. She is the president of the virtual reality and augmented reality company Technical Illusions, and worth millions.

Until I decided that my screw-ups would show me how to turn failure into an opportunity, I was constantly stuck with the bad F words. By 'failing-up' I was able to get rid of the bad business, pass on the wrong opportunities, and let go of relationships that weren't growing with me. Then, and only then, did I stop feeling like I was failing.

Feeling like a fraud is a side effect of fear and a lack of confidence in your own success.

CONQUERING THE BIG F WORD

My mother-in-law, Cindy the Librarian, may opt to read this book, so I need to start by saying that Helen Mirren (one of her favorite actresses) endorses my use of the F-Word. Well... indirectly.

Helen Mirren, a 70-year-old actress with unquestionably impressive screen credits, told the New York Daily News at Badgley Mischka's fashion show that she regrets not telling more people to "fuck off" in her life. Her reason? Because it's empowering.

"Unfortunately, at least for my generation, growing up (we didn't say [fuck off]) and I love the fact that girls are so much more confident and outspoken than my generation were," Mirren told New York Daily News. She explained that the phrase is empowering to women especially because we're so often taught to be polite in every circumstance. "We were sort of brought up to be polite and sometimes politeness, in certain circumstances, is not what's required," she said. "You've got to have the courage to stand up for yourself occasionally when it's needed."

Here is why I believe learning to use this non-PC word is important. It forces you to accept that you had a role in your successes. We, female entrepreneurs, allow others to take advantage of us or make us feel smaller because sometimes we are unable to internalize our successes. We allow ourselves to believe that because we were given an opportunity that others weren't, our role in the success of that opportunity, is not fully our doing. This allows an annoying voice in our head to remind us after every victory that nothing we achieve is 100% earned or deserved.

It's why we allow people to make us feel guilty for being successful or as if we don't deserve the credit for being successful. Or that our success was luck. Or my favorite one: telling us how much success has changed us. It's when a very well placed FUCK OFF is appropriate.

Learning how to use your F-words correctly will help protect you from time suckers, time wasters, and negative people. When you decide that fraud, fear, and failure don't belong in your vocabulary, you gain unbelievable confidence. When you realize that sometimes it is necessary to say 'Fuck It,' you feel liberated in a way that breathes new life to your resolve and creativity. Conquering your F-words is essential to feeling successful, satisfied, and serene.

Chapter Eight

The Butterfly Baby

The most common way people give up their power is by thinking they don't have any.
—Alice Walker, author "The Color Purple"

CHANGE HAPPENS IN MOMENTS

Three months after my mother's death I was driving home for a family BBQ with Jenn. It was a beautiful summer afternoon. Jenn and I were excited to toast to our decision not to form a strategic partnership with the prestigious video house in Philadelphia. We had just landed three new big TV projects for a national mattress company, a hosiery company, and breast enhancement company on our own. We did it without having to rely on the prestigious boardroom. Then the phone rang while we turned the corner to the street I lived on.

"Charlie, Ava drank citronella lighter fluid. The ambulance is on their way. Come home now."

I arrived as the ambulance pulled up. Tom was holding my eleven-month-old daughter, Ava, who had white foam coming from her mouth. I took her in my arms as the paramedic opened the doors and ushered me inside the ambulance while telling Tom to follow them to the hospital.

The ambulance took off down the same road I had just driven up.

I tried to stay calm. We would be at the hospital in no time. She would be fine. Then the ambulance stopped at the end of the road.

"Why are we stopping?"

"Our ambulance is not fitted for infants. We are from the volunteer fire department. The hospital ambulance is on its way to us to meet us here. She won't make it to the hospital without the equipment they have in their rig."

I rocked her; wiping the white foam from her mouth. I began to pray harder than I ever had in my life.

Please throw up baby Ava and get the poison out of your system. Please throw up and you'll be okay. Please, God keep her safe, and I will make it up to you. Please God, help her and I will quit Synergixx and be a better mother. Please, Baby, throw up, and it will all be ok.

The angels were still watching over me, but they weren't laughing this time.

I have a vague recollection of switching ambulances and of being rushed to the local hospital and finding Tom waiting in the emergency room with the ER doctors... doctors plural. The last thing I remember before they took her into ICU was the ambulance driver saying "thank God she didn't throw up in the rig because we didn't have the equipment to keep her lungs from collapsing if she did."

What? I had begged God to make her throw up... which would have killed her. Sometimes God hears our prayers and ignores us... thankfully.

Ava was admitted to the ICU, hooked up to breathing machines, and completely sedated while her lungs tried to heal the damage inside. Her team of doctors said we would have to wait it out and see. Tom and I took shifts at the hospital. We alternated the days, working and caring for Jake on opposite days. We'd relieved each other at five o'clock, so we could both eat dinner with Jake when we had not seen him during the day. I insisted on staying through the overnight every night.

Ava was kept sedated the entire time, in a deep sleep so she would not feel the tube down her throat. It was quiet except for the beeps of the monitoring machines. I watched one baby after another come in and go out of the ICU while I waited for her to wake up. I heard another mother scream one night when she was told her baby would not be coming back. I waited every night for the morning to come.

To keep from going insane, I would work on TV infomercial scripts and answer emails surviving only on coffee. I worked around the clock – really just waiting to see if her lungs would bounce back. I forbid anyone to tell clients what I was going through or push back deadlines or even cancel a phone call. I didn't want to give any seriousness in the real world to what I was experiencing in the hospital – if THEY didn't know about it, then it couldn't be real. It was business as usual. I lost the hosiery client because it was taking too long to write the script, but otherwise I was handling my business.

I was a happy mom when in front of my almost four-year-old little boy. I was keeping it together. As the days dragged on with my daughter unconscious in a hospital bed, I mastered the art of compartmentalizing my emotions.

Brought To My Knees

One night, I found myself knelt down by the hospital bed the way my grandmother used to make me do before bed. At first, I knelt from exhaustion. Then I remained kneeling and closed my eyes. I held my hands together and held my head straight up. And I started by just listening to the sounds of the room. I made it only a few minutes this first night before I thought "this is stupid" and got up. The next night as I sat by her bed in the hospital chair with hands folded in prayer; something forced me to my knees again. And this time, it was five minutes. I continued to kneel each night not understanding why until a week later, while kneeling, I asked myself "How will I feel if my baby

doesn't wake up?" It was the most honest question I could ask. It was a question I had been too afraid to ask God ever before. It was a question I didn't want an answer too. But on this night, kneeling at the side of her bed, I kept asking myself "How will I feel if my baby doesn't wake up?" I humbled myself on my knees. I didn't have the answer, but I asked the question anyway. Then I gave thanks for my baby. I gave thanks for the experience of being her mother. I spoke to her in my mind in a way I hoped she could feel how much I loved her if she never woke up. I knelt. To this day, when I think about kneeling in front of her... I tear up as if I was still kneeling there.

FROM HUMBLE TO GRATEFUL

The next day, as I was driving to relieve Tom at the hospital, I had an idea that popped so strongly into my head that I almost drove off the road. Butterflies and Beethoven. If Ava felt pretty and inspired, she would heal faster. After spending $150 at Baby's R Us on anything that had butterflies on it and buying Baby Beethoven CDs I arrived at the hospital almost giddy. In a matter of hours, Ava was covered in butterfly tattoos. Her bare chest, her arms, her legs, and even one pretty one by her left eye. Her hospital bed covered in butterfly ribbons. A poster of butterflies above her head. A stuffed butterfly sat by her feet. I had put tiny pink headphones on her that were playing Beethoven arrangements. I was positive she felt pretty and special. This I prayed would bring my baby back. After all, when my mother felt pretty in that wedding gown, she stayed longer. It had worked for my mother. So I made Ava feel as pretty as possible. And as I stared down at her, I allowed myself to think the unthinkable, 'if she didn't wake up, would she know how much I love her?'

In the middle of the third week, Tom and I had stepped away from the hospital bed for about five minutes to grab some coffee in the cafeteria. When we reentered the ICU, we looked at the corner where Ava's bed was and saw nothing but doctors crowding her. Panicked, I raced to the bedside trying to see through the sea of green scrubs and white nurse uniforms; there must have been a dozen doctors barricading her bed. I was weak in the knees preparing myself....

"What's the matter?" I yelled. The doctors turned around smiling. "Nothing at all. We heard the butterfly baby was waking up, and we all came to see it happen."

The butterfly baby was indeed awake.

Lesson Ten: Kneel Often

As entrepreneurs, must learn how to access the power of prayer whether you believe in God 100%, sometimes, or not at all. It is a crucial and humbling experience that has a magical effect on your life.

Ladies, we forget that we are not invincible. Our egos and our intelligence make us feel stronger than we really are in the moment. We must realize this. It took me two years to write this book, and I have read this section many times in the process; each time my eyes filling with tears because I know, like I know, like I know... moments were the length of time between Ava being in my life and not... moments.

I went through many times in my life where prayer was absent. **I went through many times when I said I was praying, but truthfully I was closing my eyes asking for miracles without intention.** And then there were times when I could clearly see the benefits of my praying.

Today, I pray daily. Sometimes for a minute and other times for twenty or thirty minutes. I am always kneeling when I do it. For me, this has made all the difference.

The act of kneeling when I pray has nothing to do with a bible or religion. It has everything to with my ego. As high-powered people who live on adrenaline, risk, and reward, it is easy to fool ourselves into thinking we do not need help. Humility escapes us. When we kneel in prayer, we physically humble our body. It's hard to be cocky on our knees. When we kneel and close our eyes even for a moment, we feel child-like again.

For me, kneeling, eyes closed, with just the feeling of being a child looking up for help, puts me in a humble place. In my humility, I can focus inward and focus on what I am sincerely praying about.

Praying is not asking a deity to fix your problems. It is asking yourself to consider questions, problems, situations, people and feelings and how you should deal with them. You are praying to yourself.

You are trying to quiet all the other voices in your head and single out the one most important inside you. You are trying to have a soul conversation. You are trying to admit something very difficult. You are trying to ask for help in the most vulnerable way. You are looking to gain clarity in your confusion and strength in your weakness. You are looking to believe again.

For me, there is a difference between prayer and meditation. Meditation is a singular conversation with yourself. In prayer, you know there is someone higher than you listening to your conversation with yourself.

I have faced some pretty terrible situations in my life that have left me crumbling inside. Times when I refused to believe in a higher power. Times when I would resent God after leaving church on Sunday because I had spent that entire service sitting in the pews praying and I didn't feel any better. But once I started kneeling, I stopped crumbling inside.

Has God ever spoken back to me while I was kneeling, looking up at him? No. For me, it doesn't work that way. Kneeling in prayer is a physical position that allows me to connect to myself spiritually. I believe in God. I believe that he hears me when I pray. I don't believe he fixes my problems or sends down miracles.

I do believe in Divine intervention that comes when the spiritual universe hears your needs in your humblest of voice. **Sometimes the Divine intervention comes in meeting a person that alters your life in a positive way.** Receiving the opposite of what you thought you wanted that turns out to be what you truly needed. The feeling of peace when you get up from kneeling. It has worked miracles me. Getting through life without learning how to kneel is a rough road.

Success at the rate and intensity people like you and I seek is scary. That's why I never forget to kneel.

Chapter Nine

The Universe Speeds Up the Lesson

I come from a line of great Sicilian women, and their mentality
is to endure and push through to the other side.
—*Cyndi Lauper*, an American singer, songwriter, and actress.

In the span of five months, I had lost my mother and almost lost my daughter. Time off? Understand my feelings? Talk about it? I wasn't ready. There was work to be done, and I needed to stay focused. I didn't slow down at all. Outside of losing the hosiery account, I had kept all the other balls in my life up in the air. The colon cleansing commercial I had produced had made my client very wealthy, unlike anyone had seen before. He was having Synergixx produce new shows left and right while sending us as many calls as we could handle, and when we couldn't handle them, he forced us to expand. The campaigns were so big that my status elevated across the industry, and more and more start-up companies were sent my way, hoping I could take their products and turn them into million dollar brands. Without a plan or safety net, we grew and grew until the walls in the old Deli started to bow outward – just like my growing belly.

PREGNANT AGAIN!

"We have to expand, or we will lose control of our biggest account. Look how far this campaign has taken us." I was adamant when my father counseled me against adding another 30 call center seats and 50 employees to the call center to accommodate the colon cleansing campaign. "Besides, the new building we found is perfect, Dad."

"Charlie, if you buy the building, expand, and this guy leaves you hanging what are you going to do?" He was gentle but unwavering.

"That won't happen. His campaign will let us take on bigger campaigns." And that's how I made the decision to spend three-quarters of a million dollars on an 8,000 square foot building and relocate my Deli Call Center.

SNOWBALL TAX PREPARATION

"Charlie, she is not doing her job. I just found the documents she is preparing for the tax accountant shoved in a drawer with a package of melted pink Hostess Snowballs on them. I asked her about it, and she said it was an accident. An accident! Have you seen her desk? Has she even presented you with a monthly P/L this year? It's May!"

I ignored both Jenn and my father. They were worrying needlessly. We were growing. The head of my accounting department was very competent; just messy.

WRONG NUMBER COMPETITORS

"Charlie, we keep getting the same wrong number calling the call center. I called it back finally. It went to a competing call center. They played dumb. I think there are trying to steal business." I ignored Jenn again. We were weeks away from opening the newer, bigger call center and securing business would not be an issue if I just stayed consistent.

CLIENT INSECURITY

Sitting in the boardroom of a client I had been wooing for three months, that had enough business to make the expansion of my call center painless, I was again faced with questions about my ability to handle large scale projects. "Charlie, you have a great reputation. But I don't think we are ready to make the move to your call center yet. We want to see how you are handling the growth in a year. Doubling the size of your call center and being a new Mom is a delicate time. You may want to take it easy, and that's understandable. Let's talk in about a year after we see how everything comes out." What were they saying? I could handle giving birth and expanding a call center at the same time!

I had done it twice before. The Universe was sending me signs but was not receiving them.

BACKWARD PRIORITIES

It was three days before my 30th birthday and I was flirting on the phone with an Australian man who wanted to market knives in the US. I was flirting with this man because I was the size of a refrigerator and it felt good to have attention from a man that didn't know I was with child. I was also flirting because I had become accustomed to men not taking me seriously unless I let them have their verbal fun. I was flirting with this man so that I could gain his business. My assistant popped his head in to tell me my father was on the phone and wanted to speak with me.

"Tell him I'm on a call and I will call him when I get home in 15 minutes." I kept flirting.

Twenty-five minutes later, I was setting out take-out Chinese food on the back porch getting ready to feed Jake and Ava dinner. My home phone rang.

"Oh, Tom! Hand me the cordless. It's probably my dad. I forgot to call him back."

"Is this Charlie Fusco? "Yes."

"Is your father Norman Moss?" "Yes."

"Miss, I'm calling from Kennedy Hospital, and we normally don't like to say this over the phone but your father…"

My father…

When I arrived at the hospital, the doctors explained that my father had dialed 911 and collapsed during the call. According to the phone records, he had called 911 about three minutes after calling my office. I had been flirting with an Australian knife salesman when my father called me for help. What? My world imploded.

The doctor continued, explaining that they tried to revive him for 20 minutes but his death had been instant in their opinion; he'd had a massive aneurysm in his main heart chamber. Since he had no identification in his wallet they had not been able to identify him other than a Dunkin Donuts napkin that said 'come back soon Norman.' They also found several sticky notes with names and phone numbers on them. What?

"We tried calling all the numbers on the sticky notes, and no one had your phone number. We finally figured it out – you were the last sticky note." What?

In three months I would be signing papers on the building my father cautioned me against purchasing; I needed him to see me thrive in that building because I wanted him to be proud of me for making the decision. He wasn't supposed to die now! I was giving birth to his latest grandchild which he would never meet. I hadn't told him that I loved him. I wasn't ready to be an orphan. I was barely holding things together, and now God had made me the 'last sticky note.' What? I was finally ready to hear to the real lesson.

Clarity Comes In Many Forms

It wasn't until the day of his funeral that I understood what the Universe had tried so many times in the last two years to tell me.

Slow down and connect.

At the church ceremony, people began arriving from every corner of the county. Current employees, past employees, the owner of the local Dunkin Donuts, and the general manager of the office supply catalog that we purchased from, the family I hadn't seen in a decade, and on and on. For hours, people I didn't recognize hugged me and whispered a personal story about my father into my ear. These were people who knew my father through my business but that I had never stopped to connect with before. The church was standing room only. Tears flowed from everyone but me.

The reception held in my backyard after the funeral allowed me to play the controlled hostess.

Finally, I stopped, standing on the balcony overlooking the backyard, and observed the scene. I was holding witness. The ex-cons covered in tattoos that worked in the call center were embracing the freshman college students that worked there too; they never spoke at the office, but here they were consoling each other. The troupe of prostitutes that I had kept my distance from in the call center was reminiscing with the media buying team about my father's yellow shoes. People who we had fired, unsure if they were allowed to be there but who couldn't stay away because they loved my father so, mingled through the crowd. In my backyard, I saw hundreds of people who had been employed by my company unite to honor a man they had only just met less than two years prior.

What my father had created within my company in less than two years, I had never been able to create in double the time: connection. He had taken the time to get to know these people and appreciate who they were without judging who they were trying not to be. While I was flying around the country trying to make strangers like me, flirting with potential clients to make sure I wasn't overlooked, and working 70 hours a week to keep everything in motion, he was connecting with the people who made my company grow. The sticky notes that the hospital pulled from his wallet were all for people who worked or had worked at Synergixx. I found out that he would check in with and be a father figure to these people. My father had made orphans of us all.

OUT OF CONTROL AND IN DENIAL

You may have noticed that I hardly spoke about my business in this chapter other than to say it was growing. Let me be clear. I had cash flow, and I had clients, and we were very busy. It did not make a profitable or stable company.

The connection I have yet to make is that while I thought I was keeping everything running smoothly (while putting up a brave front through the death of my mother, the almost loss of my daughter and the sudden death of my father), I had no real idea what was going on in my business financially. I had stopped holding my financial team accountable or even looking at a monthly PL. I had stopped checking in with my clients regularly; only when needed. So I had no real idea of where they were going with their business or if it included Synergixx. I had 100 plus employees at the time but offered monthly evaluations to none of them. My business appeared stable because by bringing in new business, I could hide the loss in profit we had started to experience. The reality was that my business was out of control in many areas:

- uncontrolled growth
- acquiring long-term debt to capitalize our growth
- billing metrics were stagnant
- our payroll was not tightly managed
- we had no concise marketing message
- debt was piling up
- the competition was sneaking in
- the economy was getting weaker

I didn't feel any of it happening. I was numb and didn't know it because when you are feeling so many emotions at the same time, you stop feeling them individually. Your loss feels like your loneliness. Your loneliness feels like your anxiety. Your anxiety feels like your aggressiveness. Your aggressiveness feels like your lack of love. Your lack of love feels like you've been abandoned. And your abandonment feels like calm because your mind and spirit begin to protect themselves. I was calm in the middle of chaos.

Lesson Eleven: Compartmentalizing

Female entrepreneurs, when faced with stressful situations or straight out crisis, must learn to compartmentalize emotions. This lesson takes lots of practice to master. Compartmentalization is a short term solution to dealing with the roller coaster ride of emotions you will encounter as an entrepreneur; it helps keep you sane and prevents you from confusing real issues with unstable emotional responses. Deal with the Facts and plan the necessary Acts to get through the situation or crisis and leave your emotions to process when you have the time and space to more deeply understand your reactions to them.

I often get asked this question: "How do you deal with (insert word here: pressure, people, balance, challenges, family, etc.)?" What I'm being asked is, how I deal with these things, *all at once.*

During the last 15 years, I've lived through many critical times and tragedies. There were many times these tragedies or critical events and their corresponding emotions overlapped. To live through all of these situations, without imploding, I had to prioritize which emotions to deal with first. Learning to compartmentalize made a big difference.

Psychology defines compartmentalization as a defense mechanism or a coping strategy. Consider a doctor who is religious but has to separate her religious belief system from her daily practice at a women's health clinic. Think about going on vacation and refusing to think about work the whole time so you can enjoy family time. The extreme level being a police officer or soldier having to file away horrific events witnessed so they can keep doing the job of protecting us.

For me, put simply, it is how my mind deals with loads of crap all at the same time without impacting the good stuff in my life.

Seventy-two hours before my 30th birthday my father died suddenly. I was two and a half months away from giving birth to my third child and was in the middle of tripling the size of my company while adding over a hundred jobs in the local community and developing an illness that would soon rock my world. I was filled with so many emotions that inflamed each other as well as canceled each other out.

I learned not to force myself to deal with all the emotions that surface while the events were happening. **I didn't try to judge or even understand how I felt about each situation – I just focused on what I could control.** By compartmentalizing each situation into smaller chunks – the Facts and Acts surrounding each situation – I could create the best possible solution at the time; giving myself the space to understand my true reaction to each situation after the dust settled.

I was the last person to speak to my father before he had a heart attack while holding the phone calling me; I filed away the massive guilt. Filing away the guilt, I focused instead on all the Acts I needed to get accomplished to bury my father properly and handle his affairs. Over the next few years, I came to realize that the guilt I felt after his death had more to do with how I allowed our relationship to sour during the two years he worked at Synergixx. Yes, it took me years to process the fact that I could have been a better daughter to him. It took me longer to separate my emotions about my father. I should have been a better daughter, less focused on my individual problems, but I was also able to acknowledge that he refused to take care of himself, and his heart attack was inevitable. Had I tried to understand all these emotions immediately after his death, I would have had a nervous breakdown. I needed to allow these emotions to stay compartmentalized in my brain and seep out as they were ready so I could handle them and make sense of their message.

An example of dealing with Facts and Acts would be how I split my day into sections and organized my activities in order by the length of time to complete and by the situational urgency. In this case, I would work on my business until mid-morning, after getting the kids to school. Then I would handle my father's affairs until lunch. Back to business from lunch to dinner. Then I focused on my kids and preparing for the new baby. I worked late at night and on weekends in short spurts where I could focus on getting specific Acts accomplished. Of course, it wasn't this cut and dry, but it is how I organized it in my head so I could move through the day more efficiently and with laser focus. When an emotion I wasn't ready to deal with crept into my head I would file it away and replace it with a Fact about the situation that I could handle. When I talk to women (and men) about compartmentalizing, I get similar reactions: "you shouldn't suppress your emotions." Or "you were sacrificing yourself by not allowing the feeling to happen." OR "it sounds like you turned into a cold-hearted bitch."

Not true. Further, I think people who must experience every emotion they are feeling at the time they are feeling it, regardless of the surrounding situation, are selfish and unprofessional.

To be successful, in all areas of your life you have to be able to control your emotions, not suppress them. By compartmentalizing my emotions during the chaos around me, I gave my emotions time to settle and mature. By dealing with Facts and Acts first, I got things done while the emotions I couldn't even understand at the time were tucked away in a box in my brain.

- I didn't confuse the guilt over my father's death with my anxiety over growing the business at the same time.
- I didn't fight with my husband because I was still mad at my mother for not apologizing before she died.
- My three children saw me happily focused on their needs not wallowing in the loss of what would have been a fourth child.
- At work, my staff didn't feel anxious because they couldn't console me as I was all polite business. This allowed them to feel helpful in getting the tasks completed needed to run the business.

Imagine your brain has hundreds of boxes in it. As you move through life, imagine that you can open and close those boxes, placing only one emotion or situation in each box. As you are ready, you work on one emotion/problem at a time by opening the box and dealing with what is inside. Then you have to shut the box and open another. The emotions/problems never touch. You have a box for each of your kids, a box for your partner, a box for your business, for that family issue that won't go away, the health issue you are facing, the debt you are trying to get out of, and the new idea you are trying to birth... you get the picture. You can't mentally, emotionally, or spiritually be in all those boxes at the same time nor can you properly deal with the emotions you experience in each situation in one box alone. By opening and closing the boxes in your head, you create an emotional organization, making you more efficient at handling what's being thrown at you and better able to handle the situations. Every time I face adversity and extreme challenges, I use simple steps to keep my head on straight:

- Compartmentalize it. Isolate the FACTS from the EMOTIONS of the situation.
- Become extremely focused ACTS that will resolve the situation.
- Open and close boxes quickly - deal with it and move on.
- Don't bring issues from one situation into another.
- Don't worry about things that don't deserve a box.

Compartmentalizing has saved me from ruining some of the best things in my life. For instance, Jenn, one of my best friends on the planet, was also an employee during some very challenging times in my business. We did not see eye to eye on the solutions. As her "boss" I could force my opinion. As her friend, I wanted her buy-in. When she didn't buy-in but rather executed my directives I felt betrayed. She should be on my side all the time. She was also refusing to hang-out with me after work as we always had in the past. I put my feelings of anger about our friendship in a compartment in my brain for more than six months while we worked through the business. In that time, we did not interact on a personal level; only business. There were many times I wanted to confront her as a friend and make my emotions known but I waited. The emotions were in a box and I trusted that I was not ready to deal with them fairly.

Several months after the very difficult time in the business, my feelings towards our friendship started to change. I was in awe that she had stuck by me during these months because of the uncertainty and stress. I was appreciative that even though it was uncomfortable to come to work each day, she did so with no less effort. I felt guilty that I had put so much pressure on our friendship with no regard for her. I felt honored to be her friend. Had I confronted her months prior, it would have destroyed our friendship.

On this windy road, as a businesswoman who wants a great family and sex life, you're going to have to compartmentalize your entire life. **The stress of being a parent, running out of money, being rejected by clients, investors, vendors, lawsuits, public opinion against you or your company, how your partner is reacting to you – even trying to balance your sex life with everything else – will be overwhelming if you let it.** It is a guarantee you'll get hit by big traumatic, potentially harmful, or life-ending events, sometimes in succession. Your ability to compartmentalize, prioritize, and focus enough time on each area of your life is critical to surviving the problem and building a solution moving forward.

Chapter Ten

A Payless Mindset

Did you ever notice that the first piece of luggage on the carousel
never belongs to anyone?

**—*Erma Bombeck*, an American humorist who achieved great
popularity for her newspaper column that described suburban
home life from the mid-1960s until the late 1990s. She also
published 15 books, most of which became bestsellers.**

Poop Plungers

What do you get when you create a smash hit TV infomercial about
colon cleansing? You become the Queen of Poop!

"Charlie, we've had to call the septic guys four times already this
month because the toilets keep overflowing because our septic system
can't handle the volume our employees are creating." Jenn was now the
VP of Operations and showing me a two thousand dollar invoice from
the company who sucked the waste each week from our septic tank into
their septic truck.

"Are you saying that our toilets can't handle our employees crap?"
I burst out laughing.

"Listen, you're only here two weeks a month with all your traveling to
hotels with toilets that don't overflow. I don't expect you to understand
BUT may I point out that the reps were letting Angelina crawl around

the call center all day yesterday thinking it was really funny when she yanked on the phone cords."

"What does that have to do with this invoice?"

"If we don't start setting aside four thousand dollars a month for septic your kid is going to be crawling around in call center crap all day!" She was serious and I kept laughing.

EXPANSION

"Okay, we need a bigger building. I get it."

"No! No! No! We need to stop getting so big. This is crazy! We've become the colon cleansing capital of the world, and now we are SHITTING our way out of the building. We need to back up a little." Jenn was trying hard to make her point. I wasn't listening.

Without a business plan in place, we moved into a 20K square foot building and grew to 350 employees almost overnight. The company's payroll was a hundred thousand dollars a week. Business was booming. We went from $8M to $17M in 8 months.

DOUBTING MY OWN ABILITIES

While I seemed cavalier about expanding the business again, privately I was like a deer in headlights. At night, when everyone was asleep, and the emails stopped arriving, I would talk to myself about everything I had no idea how to handle. I told myself that I didn't have the pedigree to run a company of this size. One night, after a particularly boring David Letterman episode, I made the sole decision to hire an executive management team to run the company in my place. Almost immediately, I added half a million dollars in payroll to the company's bottom line: Call Center Director, Media Director, Finance Director, Account Executives, IT Director, Corporate Trainers, even a President.

I told everyone the reason for the expensive hiring was so I could spend more time bringing in business and grow the company even bigger. Imagine what we could do if I brought on a more experienced team to help us handle our next phase of growth. Some of the people I gave salaries and benefits that far exceeded how much money I made. I justified it by telling myself that I would end up making more money once the company stabilized. But I needed their help now to get there.

THE POOR PERSON'S VISION

I like to say that the distance between wealth and welfare is nothing but a line in the grocery store. Let me go back to go forward.

When I was younger, before junior high school, my parents had money. I remember it. The cars. The dinners. The jewelry and fur coats. The trips to Hawaii. My parents were both entrepreneurs in real estate and the movie business. My sister and I never wanted for anything. Except I wanted my parents to get a divorce because they fought nonstop and violently using expensive glassware and antiques to show the level of their anger against walls. When I turned 13, I asked my parents to get a divorce, and they agreed. The fact that they agreed so quickly wasn't a surprise to anyone. I was positive things would get less stressful at home.

One day during their initial separation, my father took me grocery shopping, and while we were in line, he began flirting with the cashier. I knew my parents were separated and going to court hearings in the process of divorce, but I never expected my father to be flirting with other women. As a child, I had no idea that my parents had stayed together for their kids. Their marriage in many ways had been over for years. His flirting was intense. I was so embarrassed standing next to him in line. I focused on the cashier's hands as she ran produce through the scanner trying to drown out her flirtation giggles with the BEEP BEEP of the register. Finally, it was time to pay. Then I saw it. My father was paying for the groceries with Food Stamps. When did we go on government assistance? When did we lose all our money? And how could he have the BALLS to flirt with this woman moments before handing her Food Stamps? I couldn't have been more embarrassed and nearly ran out of the store as he collected the receipt.

I was also positive that our financial situation was my fault – after all I had asked my parents to get a divorce.

Over the next few months, I got used to coming home to the electricity being shut off or the water being turned off for non-payment. I was no longer shocked when my father sold pieces of furniture from our house to have money for something we needed. When we needed shoes for school, I knew we were going to Payless to buy cheap shoes that would fall apart in a few months. He wouldn't think of buying shoes from anywhere but Payless. The cheaper version of everything became the family practice.

Worse, was when my father would come into some money he would spend it immediately. Money became linked in my head with 'what uses up the resources I have right now so that it can't be taken away later?' Spend it now so they can't take it later. They being the bill collectors.

Once you've experienced severe money loss or struggled without money for a long time you develop what I call a Payless Mindset. This mindset I carried with me during the first seven years of running my company. So, when our sales exceeded $17 million, not only did I not have the confidence that I could handle the money associated with the growth, I was also making decisions within the company using a Payless mentality – short term solutions that would end up costing more money in the long run.

Lesson Twelve: Give Up Money Hang-Ups

To become a fierce and fearless entrepreneur, you must identify your money hang-ups, make peace with them, and release them. Financial abundance is an intentional mindset: you either believe you are worthy and capable of financial abundance, or you do not.

My parents going bankrupt and ending up on government assistance were only a few of the factors that reinforced my Payless Mindset. I spent my high school years watching money bring out the worst in people during my parent's divorce. The lack of money in my life also became the driving force that pushed me so hard to escape my circumstances by going away to college. Then, in college, when I lost my scholarship (even though it was my fault), it further reinforced that money today would only solve the problems of today. Each paycheck I received in college was spent the same day because I needed to make sure my tomorrow happened, regardless if my future happened. As intelligent as I am, my brain focused on living in scarcity. That scarcity mentality influenced my thinking for a long time.

We all have an emotional relationship with money, and whether we acknowledge it or not, it can sabotage our decisions in the boardroom, bedroom and every room in between. Money triggers emotions: elation, fear, happiness, guilt, safety, shame, security, even depression. Until I became clear about my personal relationship with money, I repelled money. Even when I was making hundreds of thousands of dollars a year I was living in scarcity; managing my life with a Payless Mindset.

My Payless Mindset revolved around the idea that spending money for quality that would last, limited the amount of money you could spend each day. Why buy the $150 pair of high heels at Nordstrom's when I could get a pair for $14.99 at Payless? It didn't matter that the

Payless high heels would fall apart within six months, and I'd have to buy another pair. Nor did I connect the dots that in a meeting with my peers, my $14.99 high heels were one of the reasons I felt like a fraud.

Think about it. I would sit in a room with highly successful people that wanted to engage my services so they would become even more successful in their own business. They unapologetically wore their financial abundance outwardly, and I was wearing Payless pumps and hiding my feet under the table. It screwed with my head. Would they realize what I was really wearing? Would they think it is because I couldn't afford better and therefore needed the money and would settle for less? And even if they didn't notice I knew my inner critic struggled with being able to charge them top dollar for my services because I didn't yet feel I was worth top dollar. It's not superficial. It goes beyond the shoes! The same money hang-up that told me to fill my closet with cheap shoes also told me to pay other people in the company more than I was paying myself. My money hang-up was that I was not worth it.

How did this affect me in business? In my early days, on almost every project, I can honestly say that I would work 50% for free. I would bid the projects out to get the business today rather than pass on projects or bid the projects out at the right price and wait for the clients to come back to me. My Payless Mindset helped me justify that money today in the business was better than saving up for the right kind of business later.

When I traveled, I would book the cheapest flights and hotels. This often meant flying with more than one connection and on overnight flights; both wasted hours of productivity and left me physically exhausted. I would stay in hotels that were not close to the place I needed to be and didn't have necessities of a business traveler like a business office, which left me getting up extra early to find a business center somewhere else and spending more in cab fare to get where I needed to be. I would arrive home completely worn out which made me an irritable mother and wife. This existence is totally backward.

Perhaps the worst place this Payless Mindset impacted my life was with my family's security. When I was growing my business, I was always looking for ways to invest the money we made into making more money in the business. Personal savings was not a priority. We would make a profit and I would invest in new equipment that would allow us to offer a new service. When we were making significant money, I invested all our extra income in the salaries of top-level executives that would take the company to the next level. It seems at odds with a Payless Mindset except when you consider that I would go weeks without paying myself so I could afford the added payroll. I chose to cut expenses in my family life to make room for the new executives to fly to one trade show after another and stay in the best hotels. They were worth it because, in my mind, they had the pedigree I didn't. There were months when I bought groceries on credit cards. I was running a multi-million dollar company with no personal savings and loaded credit cards.

For me, I grew up with the experience that money was here today and gone tomorrow. My relationship with money was feast or famine. Growing up, the money would come into our house just as they were shutting off the electricity. I truly believed that money could burn a hole in your pocket which is why my parents stopped having any in their pockets. Spend it, or it becomes a safety hazard!

When I was fighting my way through college, I saw first-hand how quickly money came and went. When I started my company, no matter how much money I made, I believed that I had better work harder to make more tomorrow or it would be gone.

When times were very lean, I would tell myself just to hold on for one more day.

And when I started having surplus money in my personal bank account I was always giving money away because having it made me feel guilty. How weird is that? Having money made me feel guilty! It was because I thought my financial success was luck. Luck made me feel guilty that others weren't as lucky. Further, because of my relationship with money, I was susceptible to feeling embarrassed about the money I did make because I listened to the outside opinions of friends and family who were jealous.

Through the years, I've talked with business owners about their money hang-ups and have heard everything from:

- "save every dime"
- "hire someone to manage it all"
- "I'm a money making machine"
- "I always take care of my money needs first"
- "I feel guilty when I have too much money"
- "I lie about how little money I have"
- "I need to lower my fee because no one will ever pay it"
- "if my kids are comfortable that's enough"
- "I just have to close a few more deals and then I'll be okay"

Which one of these statements is OK? None of them.

For anyone, especially the entrepreneur, personal wealth is very hard to build with any kind money hang-up. A money hang-up means that instead of using money as a tool to build wealth, security, and opportunity you have an emotional and irrational reaction to money that shapes how you save and spend it. There are many types of money hang-ups.

Payless: When you spend your paycheck as soon as you get it before someone or something takes it from you. You settle for cheap, right now solutions, rather than saving and planning toward better long-term solutions. It causes you to be paranoid about things like taxes and also causes you to avoid investing.

Shop till You Drop: money equals happiness and stress relief. You overspend to create euphoria. Perhaps this is how you were shown love growing up – with things given to you. Perhaps you grew up not having enough so being able to have what you want now is comforting. Perhaps spending and the feeling it creates fills in gaps you have with relationships in your life. Whatever the reason, this money hang-up is dangerous in business.

Extreme Frugality: an obsession with bargain-hunting can wind up costing you time and opportunity. You become so wrapped up in the challenge of finding a good deal that you can lose sight of the bigger picture or miss out on opportunities that would propel you forward. Frugality is typically a behavior learned when growing up. You grow up, watching your parents control every last penny or you watch your parents squander their last penny away. Your reaction, in either case, is to be in control of each and every one of your pennies. It makes you very risk adverse which can kill the spirit of any entrepreneur. It also creates a vicious cycle for your family.

Love of Convenience: you pay a premium for convenience because you feel it is a sign of progress. If you're in a genuine rush, it's OK on occasion to grab a coffee on the go rather than brewing it at home or buy a pre-made meal rather than putting one together yourself. If it is a constant habit, then you are using convenience more like an excuse for not planning ahead which is a sign of insecurity and lack of control.

Who Needs a Plan: Perhaps growing up you were always told what to do, how to do it, and when to do it. For many, this breeds a desire for spontaneity in the adult years. Rather than feel 'put upon,' you go in the opposite direction and plan nothing. You feel in control by flying by the seat of your pants. It leads to spending without direct purpose which leads to costly financial mistakes. It is also a mindset of entrepreneurs who do not monitor their financials closely; this is fraught with risk.

Keeping Up With the Joneses: whether personally or in business, keeping up with those we feel we are in direct competition with drives poor financial habits. Why you feel you have to keep up with those around you can stem from many past experiences. It is also the easiest money hang-up to justify in business (we need to compete with them at their level to get the same clients). With this mentality, you are looking for money that allows you to 'be like them,' instead of money that allows you to build your equity.

WONDERING ABOUT YOUR MONEY HANG-UPS?

1. Does money cause you to feel discomfort?
2. Are you satisfied with your life?
3. How do you view yourself? Are you successful or struggling?
4. What are your earliest memories around money?
5. Are you able to comfortably talk about money?
6. What word best describes how you feel about wealth?
7. Do you believe you are a millionaire in waiting?

MAKING THE MENTAL SHIFT TO DESERVED ABUNDANCE

My financial mindset was totally wrong and preventing my success and long-term abundance. I never viewed personal wealth as a way to create opportunities for others. Personal wealth made me feel selfish to my employees and my extended family. It wasn't until I almost lost my business entirely, with no way to personally safeguard against it, that it hit me. The company I had built was responsible for providing the opportunity for others to advance themselves financially. I am responsible for the financial abundance, at some level, of others. It is my responsibility to run a responsible company that thrives. It is my responsibility as an entrepreneur to create abundant opportunities for others. I had to start with myself. If I live in scarcity, there will never be security for those in my company or my family.

It took some soul searching, hard truths, and severe shifts in systems, and extreme focus but I dropped my Payless Mindset and will never look back.

Here are five things I hold to be true about my relationship with money today.

Excuses are for the broke. Really… excuses are for losers. You're either going to manage your money into wealth or not. Making excuses about why you never have enough money or blaming others is just another money hang-up keeping you financially unstable. Don't ever

believe your money issues belong to anyone but you. Being broke is just a poorly executed math problem.

Start thinking long term. When thinking about how I will make money, I think long term now. I'm not about the quick buck anymore. Now, if a client does not have the ability to make me long term revenue I pass on the project. The time I spend with a short term client takes time away from another long term client that will build more revenue for the company. Now, I save up for what I truly want long term instead of getting the 'generic brand'. Don't let short-term greed or insecurity kill long-term wealth.

You get what you earn. Don't expect abundance without paying your dues. I only count on what I know I can personally earn. Don't bet on the money. Count on it by working for it. Tax refunds, bonus checks, referral fees, and other types of 'found money' are great when they happen, but you should not plan your personal wealth or your business cash flow around them.

Seek comfort and luxury. While I am not a shop-o-holic or frivolous spender (except for on rare occasions if I'm honest), I now embrace comfort and luxury because it is good for my business and my family. Follow me on this. I stopped believing that pain was the pathway to gain and recognized that the better I treated myself, the healthier, calmer, more focused, and creative I became. Both personally and in business, this made me more successful. It was simple things. Not being shoved in coach for a 5-hour plane ride with no elbow room allowed me to skip the back ache while letting me work on the plane effectively. Taking a vacation at an all-inclusive resort with my family allowed me to plan less before leaving and enjoy more the time away from the office, making me a more present mother and wife and a more focused leader upon my return. When I wasn't stressed out, overworked, working on vacation, burping up bad food, adjusting a cheap bra or debating whether I should splurge on a massage, I could focus on the longer term thinking of my business with innovation and creativity. Learning to

seek comfort and luxury was a manifestation of my growing into my intelligence, drive, smarts and hard work – deciding if I'm smart about it, I can have my cake and eat it too. When you are not afraid to indulge in luxury, it is a good barometer for how confident you are feeling about your wealth systems.

Decide you deserve wealth. If you asked me a few years ago how much money I should make in one year so that enough was enough – I would have said something vague. 'I only need enough so my kids are well taken care of and I get a vacation once a year' or maybe when I was feeling bolder, I would have answered 'one million dollars, no one needs more than one million dollars to live happily ever after each year'.

It's a difficult question for people to answer, and more than not the amount is low. Here is why.

A "normal non-entrepreneur" person looks at a wildly successful business owner and thinks, "That lady is lucky." Or "That person is a shyster." A person with a multimillionaire mindset thinks, "What's her secret?" And, "How can I do that?" Money is out there for everyone to grab. Once you start believing you deserve to be rich, you'll change your actions to make it happen.

I used to feel guilty about earning six figures until I met business executives who earned seven figures and drove their companies into the ground! They squandered not only their abundance but took away the financial security of those that helped build their idea in the first place. I have the Brains, Boobs, and Balls to succeed where they failed if I chose to… and why hadn't I chosen before?

During the shedding of my Payless Mindset, my thoughts went from "that's not for me?" to "why NOT me too?" Believing that I also deserved the wealth that reflected my hard work caused my income to soar. Changing how I manage, leverage, and invest that money allows me to create more opportunities for growth for other people. It's perfectly aligned with my Core Drivers, and that is why it worked.

- **Follow Abundance with the Intent to Share It**
- **Create Opportunity for Others Despite Personal Status**

I became secure mentally, emotionally, and on the books when I decided I deserved it. Ask me today how much money I need to make each year for enough to be enough. I have a very different answer today. Today, I see the creation of on-going wealth as a responsibility to carry out a greater mission in the world.

Consider This Personal Wealth Distribution Plan

- 50% of your income is to be used for living expenses (housing, food, clothing, vacation, kids' needs)
- 20% of your income is to be put into savings (many options on how to do this effectively)
- 10% of your income is to be put into charitable give-back (churches, foundations, scholarships, donations)
- 10% of your income should go towards funding your next entrepreneurial idea
- 5% of your income should go towards personal development (masterminds, continuing education, lifetime experiences, etc.)
- 5% of your income should go towards building luxury into your life (special items, travel, conveniences)

Consider This Business Wealth Distribution Plan

- 50% of your revenue is to run the business (payroll, operational expenses, marketing)
- 20% of your revenue should go to capitalizing future business (line of credit, growth, asset purchases)
- 15% of revenue should go back to your employees directly (raises, bonuses, paid training, team building events, benefits)
- 10% of your revenue should cover your salary as the owner/CEO
- 5% of your revenue is to be put into charitable give-back (churches, foundations, scholarships, donations)

The amount of money it takes to live in the capacity you desire needs to be adjusted to the above formulas. If you have revenues of $1M and are not able to live the lifestyle you desire for $100K a year then you need to earn more money, not give-away less to charity. Reducing your % keeps you earning less than your potential as an entrepreneur. If you can't make more than $1M in revenue to bust through your $100K salary cap then you need to: a) adjust your business model; b) create a new revenue stream; c) reduce spending in other areas; or d) all of the above. Keep your % the same so you don't cheat your growth potential.

QUICK STORY:

A woman came to see me looking for some advice on how to handle her senior manager at work. She complained that this woman was preventing her from getting "seen" in the company and taking credit for her ideas. She deserved a promotion after seven years and felt that this woman was insecure and holding her back intentionally by not representing her hard work to Upper Management. She went on in great detail and showed me a ratty, black binder, with a dingy white label, the words 'idea folder' hand written on it. It was filled with the marketing brochures she had created. She felt this quality work was being ignored by her manager, for many reasons including holding her back in the company. She asked for my advice on getting ahead in her job.

I looked at her black binder and told her to go buy a leather portfolio worth carrying around her winning ideas.

"Spend money on something with leather. Walk in with your million dollar ideas looking like a million dollars and then present them."

Her response, "I don't think spending $50 on a portfolio to replace my $2.00 binder is going to make the difference. My problem is she won't look at them and she is the reason Upper Management never looks at me either."

My response, "Why would anyone look at you or ideas that come from that broken down place. You need to stand taller and prouder with your ideas and deliver them with an energy that says 'look at me'. You can't even sit in front of me with that energy because that broke-ass, pitiful, black binder is sucking all your energy down. You look like your folder. It has literally absorbed all your resentment and forced your shoulders into a weird position. Who wants to look at that… do you even believe what's in that sad folder is a good idea anymore?"

The moral of this story is simple. Spend the difference of $48 to look like you are worth a $48K differential. You don't have to spend recklessly to get over your money issues but you do need to invest wisely in yourself, your ideas, and how you tee-up your presentations to others.

Chapter Eleven

Intense Bikini Waxing Saves Lives

The truth will set you free. But first, it will piss you off.
—*Gloria Steinem,* **writer, lecturer, political activist, and feminist organizer.**

SOMETIMES PHYSICAL PAIN IS ALL YOU HAVE LEFT

"I will tip you $100 if you can wax every hair off my vagina! Leave me bald from the belly button down and around. Right now."

Brittany Spears made headlines because she shaved her head as part of a nervous breakdown. My form of a nervous breakdown came with my first bikini wax. Brittany's cry for help was plastered in every supermarket tabloid across the country. My cry for help was private and left my lady parts itchy for weeks. The truth hurts.

My truth was that six months earlier my banker called to express his concern that my line of credit had been maxed out for more than thirty days, and he wondered if I was even aware of it. I was not.

I went to talk with my head of accounting. She was a Full Charge Book Keeper, who had recently become an ordained minister. I figured having an 'IN' with the 'Big Guy' could only help our financial department. When I approached her about my banker's phone call she said, "I thought I could fix the problem before you found out." What?

She had overextended our payables. She was leaning on the line of credit to get her caught up. *How could we be so far behind?* She assured me that as soon as the next month's receivables came in we would be caught up. When I asked her why she hadn't made me aware of the stretch on our cash flow, she gave me several reasons that looking back made no sense. But at the time, I believed. I was in denial.

After all, what did I know about running a large company? The truth was that she was incompetent and had lied to protect her job. I should have fired her on the spot. But I didn't. The truth is that I wasn't in touch with my financials.

Instead, I took responsibility for the breakdown and told her that I needed to keep a better eye on the finances. I also made her promise that she would never withhold information again or make any cash decisions outside of our weekly meetings without my written approval. She agreed. I should have made her pinky swear.

When I told Tom about it, he asked why all my managers and operations people hadn't caught this since they were there all the time. I ignored his question because I didn't want to face the answer.

Less than four months later I got a call from my banker telling me that he wanted to come in and review my account with me. He had covered our recent bounced checks but needed assurance that our aggressive cash flow issues were only temporary. *What cash flow issues?* When I brought my bookkeeper into my office again and asked her what he was talking about; how could we bounce checks with a three hundred thousand dollar credit line? Her answer was that she had maxed out the line and had not been able to replenish it as promised with new receivables because more payables had come due. She had written checks to satisfy vendor demands and had miscalculated the automatic payments that went out of our account each month. *She miscalculated? She was sorry? She thought she could handle it? She didn't want to disappoint me?* And then it hit me.

To be unable to pay down our line of credit of three hundred thousand dollars meant that we were at least another three hundred thousand dollars in debt through payables. How could I be so much in debt when I had cleared a profit the previous year of more than half a million dollars? And then it hit me again.

I had lost more than a million dollars. I looked at my bookkeeper sitting across from me with a bland expression. I signed off on her payments weekly. I had looked at the financial reports. *What had I missed? How did I lose this money?* I asked her if she had been withholding information from me. I asked her why we were in this situation when the reports she showed me weekly painted a different story. She stared at her toes. And while looking at the ground, she began to mumble the truth.

She was not withholding information. She didn't know the information. She had gotten in over her head and had not reconciled our bank account in several months nor had she locked down the PL. She had been presenting our financial documents without accounting for everything. The financials had not been audited. I hadn't noticed because we had consistent cash flow. Everything had snuck up on her. She thought she could handle it. She wanted to fix it before I found out. She didn't want to disappoint me. She was sorry. *What?*

"Charlie, you grew the business so fast you didn't give the team enough time to adjust to the accelerated growth. In my opinion, you're great at sales but unrealistic about how business works. We are all doing the best we can despite your inexperience in this leadership role. I'm sorry." She finally looked up from the ground.

"Does God know you are sorry? How can you be a minister when you lie to people? Aren't you afraid of getting hit by lightning?" I was outside of my body angry. I yelled for Jenn to come into the office immediately. As I waited the few moments for her to arrive, I glared at the bookkeeper astounded that she could run a pulpit on Sundays. Didn't they do background checks on ministers? Didn't they know she lied to their bosses?

Jenn arrived just as I began to lose my temper. "Jenn, I'm leaving. When I come back I don't want ANY sign of this woman in our building." Jenn was in shock not being privy to what I had just uncovered. As I grabbed my purse to leave, she asked me where I was going and would I be back.

"I am going to get every hair yanked out of my pussy. I'll be back when I can spread my legs and call myself a Bald Eagle!" My extreme vulgarity was meant to punish my Minister bookkeeper. I had just discovered that my business was crumbling, and I had nothing left in me but vulgarity.

THE BIKINI WAX

Up until this point, I had been numb to everything in my life. I ignored the stress and the signs that I was not on the right path. I had so many things coming at me, hitting me, confusing me, betraying me, leaving bruises on me, that I stopped feeling anything. I had been wearing a brave face for a long time. I had been numb to it all. Instinctually, I knew I had to feel pain. Something definite, clear and painful. I needed to feel real physical pain to snap out of it! I needed to feel something. Getting a bikini wax seemed to be the quickest answer. After I had left the hair salon, completely hairless underneath my pants, I went home where Tom was eating lunch.

BALD BREAKDOWN

"Oooh, baby you came home for an afternoon romp!" He had a playful smile as he laid down his book.

"I just got a bikini wax because I just bankrupted us!"

"You lost me at bikini wax…"

"No, no, no… I think I just bankrupted us… everything… I totally screwed it all up…" Then I began to cry and hyperventilate at the same time. I was inconsolable. Over the next half hour, Tom got me to calm down and tell him the story in a way he could understand. When I finished, I began to feel my eyes swell again with tears – a feeling so strange to me because I never cried, not even when my parents died.

"It isn't fair. I worked so hard to grow this company. It isn't fair that I hired people smarter than me to run it and now I'm bankrupting us because I'm such an idiot. I have no idea what I am going to do…" I was beginning to hyperventilate again. Then Tom did what Tom does best. He popped my self-pity bubble.

"Listen, we've been talking about this for a half hour plus. The way I see it, you have two options. Call Jenn at the office right now and tell her to let everyone go and shut the place down tomorrow. Or suck it up. You screwed up. Go back to work and figure out how to fix it. You failed but you can still turn it around, if you want. Sorry, I can't stay here while you cry about it. I have to go pick up the kids, and they shouldn't see you like this, so make your decision see before I come back." **He wasn't being mean. He was just not letting me play possum.**

Lesson Thirteen: Treat Your Lover like Gold

You might expect this next lesson to be about how to escape bankruptcy with spreadsheets. That lesson is still coming. Here is a lesson I think is more important to an entrepreneur in any time of crisis.

We, women entrepreneurs, are exciting creatures, but we are not always a joy to be around. For this reason, we must find ways to treat our Lover like gold, as often as possible.

I say lover specifically, because he/she is the person you chose to be intimate with in more ways than just physical; often your lover is your selfish-confidant, your crying post, and the replacement for the enemy you don't want to face. **Married or not, your lover is the only person that you allow to see you in the most naked of ways.**

Entrepreneurship is fraught with crisis (so is parenthood by the way), so understanding this is key. The crisis is better handled when you have a lover (or at the very least your ultimate confidant) by your side – and not because they will help get out of crisis, exactly. This person is the one who knows you so intimately that they know when it is time to cry uncle on your behalf – not because they understand your business, but because they understand your body language and your unspoken words. They push you and stand by you at the same time.

For you, it may be your husband, a boyfriend or a girlfriend… doesn't matter in the end… anyone who chooses to love you in this way is doomed to get treated terribly by you! Why?

Our ambition and drive get the better of us. We push so hard to make it all happen that we take for granted that the passionate flame between our lover and us can get burned out.

In my case, I had just told my husband that we were facing bankruptcy because I mismanaged the company he allowed me to build on the back of our marriage for the last ten years. All our savings drained, our family stability in question, the arguments over loaning the company even more money, the late nights with a laptop in bed between us, the constant traveling, the rushed soccer games, the pecks on the cheek running out the door… he had endured all of it for ten years. He had done more than endure. He had supported me in every way possible. Now, when the worst possible outcome was looming in front of him because of me, he was calm and going to pick up the kids. 90% of this speaks to the type of man I married. I am hopeful 10% of it speaks to the fact that I have tried to make sure that as often as possible I let him know how valuable and important he is to me. That because of him I had the freedom to be the entrepreneur I was called to be. It is why, even when it feels silly or unnecessary, I actively do things to make him feel how important he is in my life.

On that day in the kitchen, my lover could have looked at my pitiful, crying self, and taken the opportunity to put an end to it all. He could have succumbed to my emotional breakdown and encouraged me through words or silence to accept defeat. Who would blame him? The roller coaster ride would finally be over. He could have ended our relationship. Instead, he sized me up. My body language, my words, my lack of words… and he made the call for me. He knew that given the two options he provided I would choose the one that was true to my Core Drivers. It was in his phrasing:

"…You failed but you can still turn it around, if you want. Sorry, I can't stay here while you cry about it. I have to go pick up the kids, and they shouldn't see you like this…"

Only a Lover who has been treated like gold stays so sharply invested in you… even when you are the farthest version of what he fell in love with originally. Can you see why acknowledging this person in your life is so fundamentally crucial to your success?

What's Gold Treatment?

You're not reading this book because I sugar coat things, so here it goes! The best place to start is in bed! Man or woman, your lover, collects your gold first and foremost in bed! Otherwise, your lover is really a BFF, and that's a whole different relationship. I'm a big believer in just shut up and say YES – even when you're mad (especially when you are mad). Why? He/she wasn't in the mood for your last tirade, your constant rambling about business, your hectic schedule, your risk taking, and your constant desire to be the soccer mom and the queen of the boardroom at the same time, or the fact that you talk about YOU more than anything else. He/she did not tell you "NO" when you embarked on this 'all at the same time' journey. He/she didn't say NO when you took another risk. The word NO didn't come out of his/her mouth when your unrealistic idea was still in its infancy stage. Therefore, even when you're not in the mood, suck it up and make them feel like they are more important than everything outside the bedroom. **Think like a man! There is no bad sex… just sex and escalating levels of better sex.**

You need to be consciously affectionate towards your lover in person and when away. Entrepreneurs become singularly focused on our ideas and our businesses. It's in our DNA. We can become very aloof and seemingly disinterested when we are just hyper focusing. It's why you need to plan actively to show your affection, desire and appreciation to your lover as often as possible.

OUTSIDE OF THE BEDROOM:

- make date night a priority – dress the part
- STOP wearing sweatpants around the house – your lover deserves better
- become a specialist in well thought out, kick-butt birthday gifts, that are worthy of being bragged about in the locker room
- send sexy text messages daily
- call him/her on the phone to just say hi
- brag about him/her in front of friends so that he/she blushes and friends offer homage
- ask about his/her day and care about the answer
- cancel your meeting to go to his/her business thing wearing a kick-ass outfit – be the supportive arm candy

- kiss him/her often in front of your children
- take care of hi/her parents and extended family
- desire his/her success as much as you desire your own
- when he/she asks for help drop everything and react
- say 'I'm sorry' even when it is not your fault

Behind every successful female entrepreneur is the person unique enough to stick around for the crazy journey. For that, they deserve to be treated like gold.

SIDEBAR

Let me take you away from the main storyline for a moment to interject some levity to illustrate that Brains, Boobs, and Balls can sometimes gang up on us, transforming us into becoming Dumb, Dorky, and Desperate. It's a side effect, I'm convinced. I offer you an intimate glimpse into how I attempt to "treat him like Gold."

I remember when I discovered the website. It was a Thursday. I know because I was able to overnight the product for Friday delivery in what would be my most daring, sexy CEO stunt in years. Yes, I was fighting my way back from the brink of bankruptcy and everything in my life was extremely serious but I still made time for play. And this website was the key. It had this incredible picture of a woman covered from head to toe, smiling, with what appeared to be yellow paint. This paint was form fitting and hugged every curve of her body like a Cat Woman costume. Even my post-three-baby body would look good in this. It was a great discovery.

I had found luxury, edible, Insta-dry, contouring gel – safe for use on the entire body – and it came in three flavors. Sinful Chocolate, Strawberry Bubble Gum, and Hawaiian Pineapple. Let's transport to Hawaii!

As I tell you the rest, please keep in mind that I have a weakness for not following directions.

My Hawaiian Pineapple adventure arrived before five o'clock, the kids were all gone until Sunday, and Tom called to say he was on his way home. I had thirty minutes to apply and surprise my husband with perfectly contoured curves that tasted like tropical sunshine!

It dried instantly alright. It looked like latex paint had been spilled all over my body. It was yellow. And it did smell like pineapple. That's where the packaging promises end. About two minutes after applying the contouring gel, and it drying, I begin to feel a prickly, cooling sensation from head to toe.

How do you itch this stuff without smearing it?

The prickly, cooling sensation quickly changed into an icy-hot body bag that had every inch of my body in tropical torture. I grabbed the box and read the instructions as a small white packet fell out of the box. **"Generously apply Talc powder to the area of application before** applying contouring gel to avoid skin irritation."

As it settled in my mind that I had Insta-dried myself into torture trap, I ripped open the white bag and begin rubbing Talc powder all over to neutralize the pineapple flames burning my skin off.

I heard Tom's voice coming down the hall. I hobble into the bathroom while tearing at the yellow gel and throwing wads of it to the floor; leaving a trail. I was completely desperate to get it all off, but still very vain so that I wouldn't ask for help.

"Honey? Are you alright?"

"Aha." I tried to sound desperately sexy while not being discovered. "Whatcha up to. What's all this stuff on the floor?"

"Sorry, just trying out a new wax to get rid of body hair. I'll clean it up."

I had half the dried contouring gel off my body and had started to notice red welts forming where I had ripped it off. My entire body felt like I had dipped it in acid. The sound of my voice must not have been too sexy or convincing because suddenly Tom was in the bathroom aghast at the scene. I was one part Leper and one part melted Big Bird, and there was yellow, Insta-dry gel stuck to the walls. Everything smelled like pineapples.

I survived. And Tom waited three days for my skin to return to its normal taste and coloring before he spoke of the incident.

"I'm going to the store. Can I trust you to be home alone? Or will I come back to you drowning in a vat of hot sauce again?" He laughed his way out of the house. I consoled myself that it had been the perfect plan… if only the product hadn't misbehaved.

Treating your Lover like Gold can sometimes have side effects!

WHAT IF DON'T HAVE A LOVER?

Ladies, you may not always have someone in your life that you consider a lover. But each day that you don't, you should be actively sending signs in to the Universe that you are open to one. I have heard too many women say that they are *"taking a break from dating."* What does that mean? You are so busy that making personal connections that could lead to something greater must be put on hold? Or I've heard women say that they are *" keeping things casual so they can stay focused on what is important."* What does that mean? You think you have the luxury of time to find a soulful connection to someone else? Or I've heard women say, *"I want someone to choose me for who I am on the inside."* This is said as an excuse for taking the time to create an exciting physical form that you present to the world every day.

Stop taking your life for granted. Stop being so selective about who you allow to get close to you. Stop pretending that you wouldn't love to have someone to cuddle with after a long day. Or someone to wish good morning to everyday. We crave intimacy and at the same time successful women shy away from intimacy.

You lover doesn't have to be forever. You can have many lovers in life. You should. Be open to the attention this type of person – the one that will give you this intimacy — has to enrich your world with temporarily or permanently.

Chapter Twelve

Now What?

I never dreamed about success. I worked for it.
—*Estée Lauder*

Licking My Wounds

I was alone in the kitchen. My lady parts and eyes equally swollen and my soul devastated. I felt betrayed. I sat considering my options. I had been kicked in the gut so hard that it should be okay to fall and not get back up. It had been a long and exhaustive sixteen years since high school. I had been running so fast to keep everything going I was out of oxygen. I felt alone because the decision to move forward or backward was 300% mine to make. No one could understand how I had gotten to this point or see how I would move past this point. Neither could I. I returned to the office and found Jenn sitting at my desk. She just looked at me blankly. She knew what was happening. She knew our options were minimal. She was my best friend, and she knew I had taken us down this path. She looked devastated.

This is when it hit me. People depended on this company for their livelihood. I had put us all in danger because I was pretending to be an entrepreneur and CEO but I wasn't taking full responsibility for the outcome.

What were my options? Close the doors and file bankruptcy leaving hundreds of people unemployed? Stay open and try to grow money from blank checks in little plastic cups like they do potatoes in science class? I did consider this last option for a few minutes because I was still licking my wounds.

I decided the potato idea was not going to work. Instead, I decided to repeat the decision I had made in Boston about a decade before when I lost my scholarship. My plan back then was to work hard for six months to pay my tuition until the financial aid started. I would do the same at Synergixx. I would take the next six months and through hard work, I would figure out ways to keep us operational while generating enough new business to get us out of this mess. My entire life depended on it, so it seemed like giving it the old college try was the right thing to do.

My team was not buying my unrealistic vision this time. "Charlie, there is no way we can earn our way out of this. We have to face the reality that we can't recover."

"This is crazy. There is no way to make this happen."

I called a meeting with my banker of ten years and asked for a bridge loan to stop the bleeding. I was relying on our perfect banking record up until this point to make the deal.

"Charlie, the bank cannot see how you can get through this. We can't realistically extend you more credit given what we are seeing."

I took my executive team to meet with my tax attorney and discuss solutions.

"Charlie, as your attorney, I have to say that bankruptcy is a good option. Honestly, I've never seen a company make it through a situation like yours. You can rebuild after filing. Companies do it all the time." "Charlie, we agree with the attorney. We think you are too close to the situation. Too emotionally involved to see the reality. We vote for bankruptcy. It's not that bad to start over."

Why couldn't they see my plan would work? Why couldn't they understand that I was committed to making it work? Why was it okay with everyone to throw in the towel without a fight? Why couldn't they see it my way?

I hadn't sold them on my unrealistic vision for our future.

Lesson Fourteen: Prepare to Feel Alone

Entrepreneurs must be mentally, physically and spiritually comfortable with feeling ALONE for long periods of time – with only yourself for validation and motivation. It's the key to breakthrough.

Have you ever really listened to the crowd-pleasing theme song from the hit TV Sitcom Cheers? It's not so cheery.

> *Making your way in the world today*
> *Takes everything you've got;*
> *Taking a break from all your worries*
> *Sure, would help a lot.*
> *Wouldn't you like to get away?*
> *All those nights when you've got no lights,*
> *The check is in the mail;*
> *And your little angel*
> *Hung the cat up by its tail;*
> *And your third fiancé didn't show;*
> *Sometimes you want to go*
> *Where everybody knows your name,*
> *And they're always glad you came;*
> *You want to be where you can see;*
> *Our troubles are all the same;*
> *You want to be where everybody knows your name.*

Being an entrepreneur is overwhelming. You feel isolated often. Going to 'where everybody knows your name' is all you dream about. Feeling alone is almost suffocating.

I'm not talking about feeling lonely. Lonely is as fleeting as PMS symptoms. I'm talking about the soul-sucking knot in your stomach, oxygen-depriving feeling that comes when you can clearly see you have to walk in a certain direction, and to get there you have to do it alone. No one can see the path you are choosing. Feeling of alone is so overwhelming that you think about choosing a different path, even though you know it won't take you where you truly belong. You feel so alone that you're willing to walk away from your destined path in exchange for one person who will say "they're always glad you came."

Feeling alone is not the same as loneliness. The cure for loneliness is companionship. The cure for feeling alone requires a breakthrough. When I made the decision to save my company, it made enemies of friends, strangers from confidants, and opportunists materialized. I had made the decision to 'make everything right' and no one could see it as a potential reality. Worse, no one outside of perhaps my husband believed I even believed myself. I was alone in my vision. I was desperate.

What I didn't realize is that desperate people look just like successful people.

As entrepreneurs, it is so challenging to explain the pressure and the fears we are experiencing, so we stay silent. If you've ever run a business, you can relate to that moment when you lost your company's "scholarship" and had to find creative ways to stay afloat without letting your employees, customers, or closest family members know how close to losing it all you really were. You feel like you are "dancing in a cage" with everyone surrounding you having a great time while you feel ashamed of how your business got to this vulnerable place. Or perhaps your "alone" came when you were trying to birth a concept, an idea, or follow your passion and everyone around you said it couldn't be done – or worse, didn't even understand what you were trying to do.

As an entrepreneur, feeling alone comes and goes often. You bring this feeling into your relationships too. In my case, I would be lying next to my husband and try to be invisible because I didn't want him to ask me what was wrong. The fact that I couldn't make him understand my fears would make me feel more alone. All he saw was me pulling away from him for no apparent reason.

Feeling alone is terrible, so we run from it. Feeling alone also has a lifespan. We humans are not built to live with this feeling long term, so we will find a way to get rid of the feeling. I've met so many women who have taken on mismatched business partners because they didn't want to feel alone in business. I've spoken to hundreds of women who have settled into personal relationships that are toxic because they fear feeling alone more than the toxicity. Worse are the women I've met that have given up on their dreams because the alone part of the dream was too overwhelming. Guess what? Feeling totally alone is part of the journey. You have to experience it and live through it.

Work Towards Breakthrough Alone

Feeling alone means you are on the path to a breakthrough. To facilitate the breakthrough, you need to keep your alone to yourself. Why?

- Talking about it allows the opinions of others to sway your thoughts and potentially derail your breakthrough.
- Talking about it requires you to suck others into partially formed ideas that are surrounded by anxiety and uncertainty. The person has to internalize these feelings with no power to affect the outcome. That's selfish.
- Talking with others about why you are feeling alone in your current situation delays how long you will stay in that place. Others will pat you on the back, tell you that you are going to be fine, and may even tell you that the path you are choosing is the right one – they will in the most caring way try to make you feel comfortable about your situation. It will not lead to a breakthrough.

Here's an unpopular opinion. I don't think women should miss work because they have menstrual cramps. Down some aspirin and deal with it, because the cramps will pass in a few days and life must continue despite the pain. Yes, I just likened the feeling of alone while searching for a breakthrough to menstrual cramps. It's your private journey stop trying to drag others into it with you. Why? It is pointless.

When seeking a breakthrough, our vision and our temporary struggle is so unique to us that others really can't see it. And why should they? **If you are an entrepreneur, you live a life that others would never consider, so trying to talk to them about your unique emotions creates even more space between you.** If you are feeling alone in a personal relationship how can you fairly describe your feelings and ask for advice to someone who will never feel the same way. You are asking for the impossible because you don't like feeling alone. If you are not willing to go to the deepest place to birth your idea or support your passions, then why bother.

I alone chose the ridiculously hard path to resurrect my business from the ashes. I alone decided how it would be done and made the tough choices for it to work. I alone suffered the backlash. And when the light became visible, and those around me began to gather round and see it too, I alone assured them I would not lead them down the wrong path again. **Feeling alone until you have a breakthrough is how you learn to be a leader.**

Here's how I work through my alone periods. My strategy is to say out loud:

"I feel totally alone because I'm working for something I alone believe in. I'll be fine soon."

It sounds too simple, right. It works. Just do it repeatedly. Then, rather than come up with distractions when I feel alone, I ask myself why I feel this way. I dig deep. I will write myself a letter about why I feel alone and why the things that are making me feel alone are worth it. Sometimes, the letter looks like a To Do List. Other times, a journal entry. And sometimes, it looks like exactly what it is – a cocktail napkin absorbing all my issues in black pen.

When you restrict outside opinions and force yourself to justify your feeling of "alone," in written form, it makes you think differently and more honestly.

Admitting you are going through it and then writing down the random thoughts associated with this period brings shape to your indescribable situation. It is important that when you feel so alone, you remind yourself that your ideas, initiatives and involvements are working towards a greater reward. Think about the unique life you are living and why it is by your own design. Your biggest breakthroughs come when you are at peace with being completely alone.

Chapter Thirteen

Pull Up Your Big Girl Panties

Don't limit yourself. Many people limit themselves to what they think they can do. You can go as far as your mind lets you. What you believe, remember, you can achieve.
—Mary Kay Ash, American businesswoman and founder of Mary Kay Cosmetics, Inc.

PULL UP YOUR BIG GIRL PANTIES

How did I go from running a multi-million dollar company to losing almost four million dollars and being days away from bankruptcy? I screwed up. There is not much else to blame it on. I was moving too fast; not paying enough attention. Refused to ask for help. Allowed others to make decisions for me who were simply not qualified for the roles I put them in. That's how I lost it. I can't take credit for my success if I don't acknowledge my role in the failures. How's that for some big girl wisdom?

I went back and thought about some of my Core Drivers. How would choosing the easy route of bankruptcy support them?

1. **Follow Love not Security**
    I loved the company I had built and despite the financial issues it still produced a great product.

2. **Follow Passion not Success**

   I was still passionate about the company and the people who built it.

3. **Be Kind**

   Hundreds of people were on the payroll. I could buy time by rapidly downsizing the people who had nothing to do with our financial problems. To buy the time I would have to be ruthless. This was the opposite of kind.

4. **Marry and Stay Married Happily – Forever**

   I had no idea what bankruptcy would do to my marriage. How it would change his trust in me or the family dynamics. I wasn't willing to gamble on my marriage if I wasn't forced to.

5. **Inspire my Children by Example**

   What message was I sending my children if I gave up without trying? What level of responsibility was I showing them by using business laws to avoid my debts?

6. **Give my Children a Premium Education**

   By downsizing or going out of business, I would be affecting my child's education indefinitely.

7. **Always be My Own Boss**

   Would I be brave enough to run another company again after failing at this one? I wasn't sure.

8. **Take Risks in Everything**

   Trying to earn our way out of debt seemed risky but so was any option. Risk didn't scare me anymore.

9. **Do Things that Scare Me** Check!

I needed to make some Activating Decisions and some Balancing Decisions, but I resolved to make it happen.

After the visit to my tax attorney, where almost every member of my team agreed with him, not me, that the only realistic option was bankruptcy, I had serious decisions to make. Bankruptcy didn't work for me. **So I decided to change my reality instead. I created an Unrealistic Recovery Plan, which included more than 50 steps/actions.**

Here are a few:

- If you didn't believe we could earn our way out of debt as a unified company, then there was no place for you in my recovery plan. Eliminating the non-believing, upper-level management people saved me three hundred thousand dollars right off the top.
- If you weren't ready to change how you were doing work in the company, we would just keep repeating mistakes and that had no place in my recovery plan. It allowed me identify my weak links and replace them with stronger candidates.
- If the bank couldn't see how we could earn our way out of the situation, then the spreadsheets I had put together would need to be redone to execute my plan. It allowed me to get very good at selling our recovery story in ways the bank could respect.
- Rather than suffer through the solutions on my own, I reached out to mentors with financial experience and aired my dirty laundry. I would not let pride impact my recovery plan.
- I created new revenue streams for the company using products and services we already sold to increase profit.
- I would use my decade plus of steady business to gain help from my vendors.
- I created detailed spreadsheets of every aspect of my business and used them daily to double check the efforts and results of every member of my team.
- I reached out to companies and tried to buy their assets for a percentage of future sales so that I could generate better cash flow in real time.
- I renegotiated the terms I had on my bills with vendors, banks, and credit card companies.

Over the next eighteen months, I became intimately involved in my business. I got specific details on every area of my company from everyone who worked for me. I spoke to every vendor about our situation and assured them they would be paid if they would work with me. I scheduled meetings with my banker regularly to keep him calm.

I learned that banks don't want you to fail, they just need reassurance your situation won't get worse. I discovered that banks were very flexible when spoken to the right way. Credit card companies are actually push-overs if you know what to say.

I had hard conversations with my team. We tightened up every part of the operation. We put our heads down and focused on new business to support our existing revenue streams.

It would be a long, hard eighteen months but if my predictions were correct we'd be back on track. It was completely unrealistic for everyone involved, and I was determined to make it happen anyway. **It was going to suck. This I knew.**

I decided to put on my big girl panties for the first time.

Lesson Fifteen: Master Excel to Gain Clarity

If you can't use Excel like a Ninja – take a class. Entrepreneurs must understand the math of business. Learning how to explain the positives and negatives of our ideas and challenges using quantifiable numbers is key. Working with quantifiable data personally and tactilely makes you a fierce problem solver.

I could lie to you and say that long term relationships, calling in favors, and spikes in new business got us out of hot water, but the truth is that Excel spreadsheets were the savior of this story.

When I decided to save my company, I had to understand my company without emotion. Excel is emotionless. I spent countless hours organizing, verifying, double checking and forecasting using Excel spreadsheets that I created and refined. When I got those correct, I would send the spreadsheets to my bank and vendors. Based on their reactions to the universal language of math, I would know how to change my strategy to be successful in my recovery plan. I became so good at telling the story of my past, present, and future in an Excel spreadsheet that when I was at my lowest point in business, other companies and people wanted to get attached at the hip with me because of the mathematical probability of huge success that I could forecast on a spreadsheet. Why?

Even in what we entrepreneurs see as failure, others see as an opportunity. **In business, the difference between success and failure is a few zeros and days on a calendar. With the right spreadsheet, you can see a future is bright even though your current situation seems dark.** Don't get me wrong; you'd better be able to execute on the spreadsheet you put together. You have to be able to deliver on your plan. Execution is king. Yet, no matter how terrible the problem looks, Excel can help you make it look 'doable'.

Countless is the number of times that creating an Excel spreadsheet has changed my perspective on a problem, given me the courage to execute tough decisions, provided clarity in uncertain situations, while helping to check my emotions during times of stress and panic. It has also served as a tool for communicating business ideas using the universal language of math. While fondling data in a dynamic Excel spreadsheet is not the sexiest tool a woman can use to change her moods, it is certainly one that saves the day when used correctly.

Several ways I've used Excel spreadsheets to solve impossible problems are:

- Validating my P&L and Balance Sheet after my bookkeeper was fired; discovering the errors
- Gaining extensions on bank loans based on revenue projections
- Negotiating terms of sale with vendors; better discounts and payment options by illustrating the volume we would bring to them
- Creating sustainable cash flow in the business by better organizing my receivables and payable
- Presenting a solid financial health check to outside auditors that didn't understand the nuances of my business
- Securing short term financing options from outside investors
- Acquiring new equipment when I needed it, instead of when we could afford it, by juggling cash temporarily
- Increasing my savings by understanding my profit cycle
- Convincing American Express to extend a $600K charge for 60-days so I could make strategic moves within my industry

Excel allows you to find clarity in an uncertain future. Whenever I get anxious about finances, worried about cash flow, or stressed about an unforeseen impact on my business, I spend hours creating interactive spreadsheets that allow me to work through scenarios and solutions.

I have been able to avoid huge errors in cash management, prevent premature judgment errors, and adjust pricing models in enough time to save profits in my business. The fact that I can use all the features in Excel to organize my thoughts, predictions, and concerns into a visual format make it much more palatable to ride out tough times in business.

The secret to this lesson is that YOU must create and manipulate the spreadsheets personally. Having them created for you defeats the purpose, hides mistakes, and limits your own dynamic entrepreneurial thinking. When you learn how to create a spreadsheet for your business or personal life you will ask the right questions and provide the details others do not know. You will also physically feel the confidence or lack of confidence in your planning with each cell you fill-in. It is tactile problem solving at its best. It makes you a fearless problem solver. It teaches you the math of your particular business.

You must look at P&L's monthly (with a Balance Sheet). **You must run your business with a solid cash forecasting model.** You need to have your financials audited quarterly. You should plan every major business decision using a financial viability worksheet. You should hold your staff accountable using spreadsheets that paint a clear picture of the strengths and weaknesses of your current business. These are just a few of the key actions supported by Excel spreadsheets in my company and that have been crucial to my overall success.

Is Excel perfect? Maybe not for all scenarios, but it's a damn good tool for professionals. I run both my business and home life forecasting from an interactive Excel document. I use these documents with clients, vendors, banks, team members, and my husband to allow them to see what I'm thinking and easily talk through money issues that cause others friction. **Become an Excel Ninja! Period.**

Chapter Fourteen

Sick, Tired, & Fat

My philosophy is that not only are you responsible for your life,
but doing the best at this moment puts you in the best place for
the next moment.

—Oprah Winfrey, media proprietor

Murphy's Law

I would be lying if I said my eighteen-month recovery plan went off
without a hitch. A lot can happen in eighteen months. Not only was it
incredibly stressful to try and earn our way out of such a big cash deficit,
but we were doing it while adding workload to a severely reduced staff.
We also had no cash reserves in case of emergency. **Every step we took
forward could be three steps backward if something backfired.** We
didn't have even one step to take backward if we were to survive this
period. You've heard about Murphy and his Laws, right? During the
most fragile periods of my eighteen-month recovery plan these are some
of the things that went wrong:

- Hurricane Sandy hit New Jersey with a vengeance leaving many
  of my clients unable to pay me for months as they recovered
  from the major damage that virtually shut them down.

- The recession was in full swing and consumers weren't spending which meant clients were spending less.
- Banks were all skittish, making simple banking transactions more difficult and harder to access funds.
- The technology was changing and we had to figure out ways to purchase new equipment we couldn't afford to service the business we were securing to stay in business.
- We were cyber hacked and forced to pay more than a hundred thousand dollars between recovery and new software to get our systems secure again.
- My competitors poached employees and I didn't have enough money to counter the offers, so I had to let them go.
- Three clients in the span of ten months either went bankrupt or simply stopped paying their bills leaving us with another huge financial gap close to a million dollars.
- Given the economy, changes in consumer buying habits, and fierce competition, we were forced to lower our prices to stay competitive with major accounts.
- I had key upper management leave for more secure positions without sufficient notice to get a handle on their tasks.
- Synergixx became involved as a third party in several lawsuits and to defend ourselves we had to hire attorneys that further burned through our cash.
- And then there were the little things like replacing toilets, fixing air conditionings, and the increase in health insurance rates that we paid for our employees.

How did we survive? We offered great services that clients kept using.

I was working non-stop to keep up. I was working so many late hours because I refused to miss any kid activities during the day. I was so determined that my kids would never wake up and realize that we were not 'fine.' I wanted them to feel safe and normal. I was so focused on the recovery plan that I didn't realize I was drinking three pots of coffee a day.

SLOWED DOWN BY DISEASE

It wasn't until my scalp began to peel off, my skin became extremely dry, and I broke out in terrible acne while getting migraines routinely that I thought perhaps something was wrong with me. But I didn't get checked out. When I started struggling to get out of bed in the morning, I thought about going to the doctor and getting checked out, but stress (I made the excuse) makes you tired, so I just dealt with it.

I gained 45lbs added to the 25lbs I had yet to lose from my pregnancy three years prior. I had zero energy. My muscles ached all the time. I could barely stay awake during the day. My scalp itched all the time and my mood swings were deadly. Through extreme dieting, I lost 20 lbs, but nothing I did could affect the 55 lbs I was still carrying around in excess. I went from having an insatiable libido to never thinking about sex. These should have all been clues to focus entirely on my health. Not me. I am a kick-ass entrepreneur that is unstoppable, remember?

I finally went to a doctor in a size 20 pair of pants, terrible body aches, and barely able to keep my eyes open. Extensive blood tests over six months revealed that I had developed Hashimoto's disease. A severe case.

My endocrinologist explained that I had acquired this disorder in which the immune system turns against the body's tissues. Essentially, my immune system attacks my thyroid and "eats the hormones" my thyroid produces.

Since the thyroid gland makes the hormones that control metabolism, including my heart rate and how quickly my body uses calories, any piece of food I put in my mouth made me exhausted in the span of twenty minutes. My body can't metabolize food normally. One doctor said I had the metabolic activity of a corpse. Food is not converted for energy leaving me exhausted all the time. I was in a brain fog all day. I drank coffee around the clock just to function.

"How can I just get this disease out of nowhere?" I demanded. "Charlie, Hashimoto's can take years to develop. Common initial symptoms include extreme fatigue, anxiety, nervousness, muscle pain, depression."

"You just described being a CEO! I have a disease because I chose to run my own company? That's bullshit. This is why I haven't seen a doctor in years!" I may not have been listening too well at this point.

"It's a disease enhanced by stress. If I am giving you an educated guess, I'd say it was triggered by stress to your immune system during your last pregnancy. Was it particularly stressful?"

"Stressful? Angelina almost fell out of me she was in such a hurry to be born. I was driving in a severe thunderstorm while in labor. But nothing really out of the ordinary was stressful." I forgot to mention I was expanding my company at the time and silently dealing with the loss of my parents. I was Hashimoto screwed.

Tom was married to a menopausal alien during this period. My staff thought I was losing my mind or had achieved full BITCH status. I went to eight different doctors to try and get the right treatments. I was looking for the doctor with the magic pill. Each had his theory. I tried medications. Hormone injections. Extreme diets. Acupuncture. Combinations of all of these treatments together. It was all happening while I was trying to earn my way out of a major financial tsunami and avoid stress. This disease was the last thing God could have chosen to hand me.

With every new problem, I added to my spreadsheets and tried to forecast a solution. I called vendors and adjusted expectations. I communicated with the banks assuring them we were on top of it. I tried to ignore the fact that my team was getting smaller and smaller, and the effort we needed to put in kept getting bigger and bigger.

To be an entrepreneur, you have to be stubborn and determined. I would get through the eighteen months on plan. Nothing would get in my way. Not fatigue. Not weight gain. Not disease. Not cash flow problems. Not bill collectors. Damn it! I said I could do it.

Truth. I was totally maxed out, and it was destroying my health, but I didn't care. I didn't listen to my husband who begged me to follow my doctor's orders. My eighteen-month plan and being accessible to my kids were the only two things that mattered. **The same gene that makes us want to be entrepreneurs is also the same gene that**

makes us dangerously reckless with our own health. The Universe was knocking again.

Emergency Trip To The Hospital

Driving home one afternoon to make a kid's recital I got sharp pains in my stomach so intense I had to pull over. I barely made it home. I sat on the couch for seconds before Tom demanded we go to the hospital obviously able to see the severe pain I was in.

"Mrs. Fusco, you think you may have a bladder infection?" The admissions nurse asked a series of questions before releasing me to the waiting room.

Another ten minutes passed, and I began to sweat, and my vision became blurry. Tom insisted I needed immediate attention. The attending nurse brought us to the ER exam room. Moments began to pass.

"Mrs. Fusco, we need to make an ultrasound to rule out pregnancy because your urine sample tested positive. You could be having a miscarriage right now."

"That's impossible! I am scheduled to get a Vasectomy next week." Even in delusional pain I laughed out loud at my husband.

"Mr. Fusco, THIS would still be happening." The nurse was not amused.

Tom and I were equally surprised when the ultrasound revealed I was pregnant. My health had been so poor over the last few months and our personal time together so sporadic I didn't understand how it could be possible. And I was on the pill too.

"Mrs. Fusco, we need to get you into emergency surgery, or you run the risk of a rupture. **I need to know if you plan on having more children in the future** or if we can remove both sides of your tubes, which is what we recommend given the severity of your situation. If we remove both you understand, you can no longer bear children naturally." Literally, within thirty seconds as I was rolled into surgery, **I had to decide if I wanted ever to have another baby again while I was losing the one inside me.** Tom looked down at me. The decision was mine alone.

How did I get here?
Is this my fault? I am losing this baby because of how hard
I have been pushing my body? Because I work too much?
Is this happening because I refuse to
take medication for my disease?
Is it a boy or a girl?

I woke up from surgery and went home in what seemed like nanoseconds. My kids were quietly aware of what had happened. They tiptoed around me, waiting to read my mood. Then, three days after, my youngest, Angelina, sat next to me on the couch and asked to see where 'they took the baby from'. I wanted to explain to her that it wasn't a real baby. It was an almost baby. No, not an almost baby… an egg that wanted to be a baby but… no… it was a baby that momma just hadn't known about yet…

She looked at the red puffy skin on my belly and considered it for a moment.

"Mom, so now what are you going to do since you can't have any more babies?" She was inquisitive. I swallowed hard. I couldn't answer. "I thought we should take a vacation. When we come back, you can finish fixing Synergixx." She was definite in her opinion. I placated her with 'we'll see.'

She was relentless about her idea for a vacation, asking me daily, sometimes hourly, when we could take a vacation. She was relentless in trying to get me to see that taking a vacation with her was the only thing we should do.

"Mom, we could sit in the sand together and talk about the baby in the sunshine so it won't be so sad, okay?" Relentless.

"Once you aren't sad anymore Synergixx will be easy to fix. Okay, Mom?"

"You know Mom, you said that owning your own company meant you were the boss. Can't you tell you to go on a vacation with me?" Relentless.

And just like that, it hit me. I had fucking missed the entire point!

I was missing the most important things in life. I wasn't enjoying the life I was building with such intensity to support those around me. I was surviving for those around me. It took my six-year-old to make me see it. I was completely out of touch with myself and everything around me. I was an entrepreneur in action but not in spirit. I was a wife in action but not with my entire being. I was a mother building a secure world around her children that kept me from enjoying that world with them. I didn't admire the woman I had become.

Lesson Sixteen: Orgasm Daily

Female entrepreneurs should most definitely have at least ONE, if not more, orgasms daily. Period.

This next lesson you will 100% think comes from out of left field. I just finished telling you about how my entrepreneurial drive and business pursuits made me lose sight of what was really important while making me physically ill. Now I'm going to talk to you about orgasms. Trust me, it all comes full circle here.

Allowing bankruptcy to creep up on my business, living with an all-encompassing disease for almost three years without seeking medical help, and forgetting that I love orgasms are all very much connected. **As both women and entrepreneurs, our brains, boobs, and balls are physically connected. Our ability to use our intelligence creatively, command a physical presence, and feel the confidence to take the risks is built on a foundation of our physical well-being.** Our eventual plateau, major breakdown, or give up point is directly related to losing touch with how we feel physically on every level.

When I tell women that their success depends on their ability to orgasm daily, I get laughs, looks of disbelief, and judgmental eye rolls. When I tell women, "I'm serious, and I strive for three a day," I get 'not possible' and 'how do you have the time?' And then comes the excuses as to why having orgasms is not a priority.

As women, we continually put others first in our lives. We allow ourselves to get tired, depleted, run down, drained, exhausted, desexualized, overworked, unappreciated, numb… we forget that our mind and body are connected.

Once I took a serious look at my health and decided to focus on getting back to my former, healthy self, I realized orgasms were key. Here's why.

I've always had a high sex drive. Thankfully, so does my husband. Orgasms have never been an issue for me when I wanted one. Here's the rub. I became so unhealthy in mind, body, and spirit that going weeks without wanting one became normal. Then it became months without feeling any desire at all, and I wasn't alarmed. This is coming from a woman who gets distracted by a cool breeze or the UPS delivery guy in his summer shorts outfit! No desire? Me? And I was okay with this? I hadn't connected the dots between not desiring this physical release and my health being imbalanced. Think about this. If whenever someone needed your help or your attention, your response was:

- I'm too tired to engage right now.
- I'm too busy to deal with you right now.
- I'm not feeling well.
- I have no desire to do anything right now.
- I have a headache, so I can't help you right now.

How would these responses play out with your employees, vendors, partner, family, or friends? They wouldn't. Period. You can't say these things to your kids, employees, or clients without repercussions. And you certainly can't say them continuously to your lover without major backlash. So, why is it okay to say it to yourself when it comes to your sex drive? **A lack of physical desire is a red flag that something in your life is going haywire!** We are hot-blooded, passionate women. Female entrepreneurs burn inside. Our sex drive is like fuel coursing through our veins. You should want to have orgasms all the time!

Only girls in porn videos enjoy sex that much, right? NO!

Aren't we told that many of us naturally have trouble orgasming? Haven't you heard that we need an emotional connection in order experience physical release? Perhaps bad sexual experiences turned you off to your natural rights as a woman? Or your age and hormones are responsible for your lack of desire? All of this not true. Worse, some women have even grown up believing it is wrong.

So when we go through periods in our life not desiring orgasm we never equate it to an imbalance we need to fix; sometimes we don't even notice our desire is gone. If you have no physical desire how can you be at your creative best mentally? They are connected.

After I lost what would have been my fourth child, I didn't compartmentalize my emotions. I sat for many hours after surgery processing my emotions letting them wash over me mercilessly. I blamed myself for not taking care of my health so that my body wasn't strong enough to carry this child. I criticized myself that I couldn't even remember the last time I had sex to even get pregnant. I was sad and distant. I felt sorry for my children to have to see their mother go through this because it was not the lesson I wanted ever to teach them. I wondered if my husband secretly blamed me for not protecting our child better because he had been begging me to take care of my own health for years. I asked God if being unable to have children any longer was another lesson I needed to learn. I thought about my business and all the energy it consumed of me. Had I chosen my career over another baby unconsciously? **I wondered who I was playing the fearless entrepreneur for – me, them… who?** If my physical inability to bring this unborn child to term was so compromised how was my health affecting my three living children? When I was done feeling all these emotions, I made a decision to focus on my health first and foremost so that I could start taking control of my life again.

An Unexpected Change In Sex

I started doing all the normal things you would think of to improve my health like watching my diet, exercising, taking supplements, and trying to relax. Nothing miraculous happened except I lost a few pounds and had a little better energy. Then I discovered my health breakthrough.

In 2013, while researching a brain product for an infomercial I was producing, I read an article that orgasms made women smarter. *Hello! I want to be smarter!*

Rutgers University released data showing that sex is more powerful at strengthening the mind than any brain game. The researchers used an fMRI machine to measure blood flow to different parts of the brain. Then they had participants engage in a variety of activities from crossword puzzles to self-stimulation. They discovered that while certain mental exercises (such as crossword puzzles or Sudoku puzzles) can increase activity in parts of the brain, only orgasm increased activity across the entire brain.

If I have more sex I can think faster? Sign me up!

Another study done by a team of researchers at the University of Maryland found regular sexual activity not only allowed for neurogenesis (the creation of new brain neurons) but also improved cognitive function, potentially helping people think more clearly. *More evidence that orgasms could supercharge my brain!*

I read further. Neuroscientist Professor Barry Komisaruk, from Rutgers University, who spent years studying female sexuality, recommends mastering orgasms if you want to give your brain the ultimate power workout.

As someone who is always pushing her personal limits, the concept that I could get a mental edge by flooding my brain with the right chemicals as a result of sexual activity was intriguing. Was the fact that men have notoriously no issue with masturbation and do it often the key to why there were more men in CEO positions than women? It was a question that my competitive nature demanded an answer too. I ask you to consider the question. I researched deeper.

What I discovered is that the female orgasm sends a mighty surge of blood flowing to the brain, according to Komisaruk. The result, a dramatic increase in mental activity throughout the length and breadth of all that resistant grey matter. This was studied against normal brain games. The *New York Times* crossword, by comparison, only lights up parts of the brain — its benefits are localized. After orgasm, your entire brain is lit up.

As I read this research, I began to think about how increased brain activity would help me function better at work. If I could think faster, I could solve problems quicker, and have more time for myself to focus

on my health, my kids, and my marriage. I could make myself smarter by exercising it with orgasms. I began to see orgasms as much as a tool for success as mastering an Excel spreadsheet. I believe orgasms for female entrepreneurs are as valuable to running your company as understanding your company's financial statements. Sexy, right?

SCIENCE IS ON THE SIDE OF WOMEN

Here Are Several Facts I Uncovered:

- Researchers from Korea conducted a series of experiments on mice to see how their brain activity changed in response to sexual activity. It turns out, sex increased the mice's neurological activity for more than 24 hours after the act. That heightened brain stimulation was still present even when mice underwent stress tests after having sex.

- Dopamine, a neurochemical released during orgasm, stimulates pleasure circuits in the brain and provides a sense of well-being.

- Serotonin, a neurochemical released during orgasms, provides a sense of ease and calm, controls impulses, and aggression. Women, in general, have about 30% more serotonin than men. Women, with ovaries that make the most estrogen and progesterone, are more resistant to stress because they have more serotonin. Women with less estrogen and progesterone are more sensitive to stress and have less serotonin. Now my sexual hormones were a way to handle stress better. It was getting better and better!

- Sex, even when you don't orgasm, acts as a natural pain reliever because it causes your body to increase production of oxytocin, which is often referred to as the "love hormone." Doesn't this provide the perfect comeback to the old "not tonight honey, I have a headache?" Beverly Whipple, the professor emeritus at Rutgers University and a famed sexologist and author, reports that when women have an orgasm, pain tolerance threshold, and pain detection threshold increases significantly, by up to 74.6 percent and 106.7 percent respectively.

- Regular sex can also boost your self-esteem. For those in a monogamous relationship, studies have found that semen does contain several mood-altering hormones that can reduce depression, testosterone, estrogen, follicle-stimulating hormone, luteinizing hormone, prolactin, and several different prostaglandins. Some of these changes have been detected in a women's blood within hours of exposure to semen. I can boost my confidence at work by having more sex with my lover!

- Orgasms, not merely sex, boosts immunity because the endorphins released during orgasm have been found to stimulate immune system cells that fight disease. Researchers have found higher levels of Immunoglobulin A (helps protect against infection). I have an autoimmune disease, so I need plenty of endorphins!

- Orgasming is good for your heart too! Intercourse, depending on your level of enthusiasm, can be considered aerobic exercise, burning up to 200 calories per session. After sex, blood vessels dilate and blood pressure is then reduced. This change in blood vessel constriction may also help with tension headaches.

- Every time you reach orgasm, the hormone DHEA increases in response to sexual excitement and orgasm. DHEA is a hormone that helps keep skin healthy and even work as an antidepressant. Therefore, the added health benefit is that you will feel—and look—younger, longer.

- Orgasms make you glow! The glow of good sex is real. Women who have more sex have higher levels of estrogen, which is essential to enjoying healthier, smoother skin. It also promotes the production of collagen, which keeps the skin supple and gives you a healthy glow.

- When we are more sexually active, we give off more pheromones, the chemicals we produce to increase the interest of the opposite sex.

Okay, that was a lot of facts. Now I want you to go back and read these facts and ask yourself how these benefits would improve your

performance in a business meeting, a PTA meeting, and after dark meetings.

Clitoral Study

After reading the research, I decided to do my own "clitoral study." If orgasms could improve my brain power, decrease my stress levels, keep me calm, make me more attractive to the opposite sex, and keep me from getting sick, how would that impact the growth of my business and improve my role as a mother and wife? This question sparked my hypothesis.

I hypothesized that one orgasm a day would give me a personal advantage in my productivity. Then I thought, what if I had 3X my brain power, 3X less stress, and 3X more energy – what could I accomplish then? I embarked on a crazy experiment. For one year, I would have three orgasms a day. I looked at this similar to going on a strict diet or committing to a strict workout. When athletes want to go to the Olympics, they train several times a day, every day, and eat very strictly. I would treat orgasms like I was training for the Olympics. For one year I would make it a priority to have three orgasms a day. I treated it like a job.

I know this sounds comical, but it truly wasn't very easy. I had to learn about my body even more than I already did. I had to monitor what I ate more strictly because of my disease and the effect it has on libido. I had to exercise more than usual to have enough energy to combat my diseased energy levels. I had to schedule O-times. I had to get mentally creative to keep me mentally engaged, as well as physically engaged. I had to be very present when I was with my husband, and I had to master the art of self-pleasure when I wasn't. I learned to cut myself some slack. Some days, it was a fun adventure to orgasm three times. Other days, it seemed like a chore I couldn't get done. Some days, I couldn't get past two. And not all the orgasms were equally as great. But I stuck to my three a day regimen for an entire year regardless if I was at home or on the road. I was determined to keep the hormones flowing to my brain. I was warrior-like about it.

THE RESULT?

While you could argue that what I'm about to tell you could have happened without the surge of orgasmic chemicals to my brain, I will argue that **I accomplished more in these twelve months physically than my doctors could force with medication and financially more than my accountant could believe.**

- First, my business grew $5 million dollars in gross revenue during this year.
- I reduced about 1.2 million dollars of business debt.
- I was able to stop the up-and-down cycle of medication I was on for my Hashimoto's disease.
- I lost 45 pounds.
- I was sick only once that year, and it was only about three days.
- My husband and I hardly exchanged a negative word and started acting like newlyweds again.
- I found it easier to stop working at night because I was less stressed about work and enjoyed my kids more.
- I created three new revenue channels in my business.
- Rekindled two relationships with women I had lost touch with who became my best friends again.
- Had meaningful conversations with Richard Branson, Goldie Hawn, Oprah Winfrey, and John Gray because they noticed me in a crowd.
- I had the energy to start writing this book at night and on weekends.
- We bought our dream home.
- I amassed significant personal savings for the first time since I started my business.
- My kids entered private school.

- I joined a group of incredible entrepreneurs and started traveling the country doing once in a lifetime things.
- I was able to put on lingerie for the first time in eight years, look in the mirror, and say, "I'd definitely want to sleep with me!" I am happy and laugh all the time.

All this from having three orgasms a day? Yes. When you prioritize yourself in a healthy way, you allow yourself to serve more people in life. Being in touch with ourselves (excuse the pun) is in one way meditative, and other ways like developing a performance advantage. To have three orgasms a day, even one a day, takes discipline, focus, self-reflection, creativity, and respect for yourself. Also, the benefits of orgasming regularly help you succeed within many of the lessons I've outlined:

1. **Brains** – regularly flooding your brain with hormones produced during/after orgasm make you smarter
2. **Balls** – these same hormones boost your confidence
3. **Boobs** – the same hormones make you look and feel younger and respect your body's power
4. **Committing to Your 'Why's** – is easier when you are euphoric
5. **Play, Passion, Progress** – obvious connection
6. **Parenthood** – orgasm can make babies and help you tolerate your kids when it gets overwhelming
7. **Unrealistic Salesman** – the chemicals flooding your body from daily orgasms will keep you engaged and passionate
8. **Falling in love** – your body will be flooded with happy hormones and your pheromones will be off the charts
9. **Compartmentalizing** – physical release keeps your mind off things you are not ready to deal with by replacing emotions with energetic feelings of self-love
10. **"F" Words** – if you are chemically balanced, less stressed and more confident the F-words take on new meanings

Flooding your body with feel good, stress relieving, and brain stimulating hormones every day becomes like a vitamin your body craves. So, why aren't doctors and health enthusiasts telling every woman to add orgasms to her daily diet?

When I talk to groups about this aspect of my success, I get a bevy of mixed responses. The biggest being "How do you have the time?" Come on ladies, if you can't make time for a quickie orgasm you have big problems. You are the CEO of your entire life. Schedule your orgasms! Don't overcomplicate it. You take a shower every day – don't waste this alone time!

Another question I get from both men and women is "What if you aren't in the mood with your partner?" Well, that's a loaded question. Assuming you are overall happy with your partner but perhaps just going through a blah period, my answer is 'just do it.' You don't always feel like going to the gym, but when you force yourself, it always feels better after. The more you work out, the more you'll crave it and see the benefits. Besides, there is something sexy about hearing a woman say "I have no desire to make love to you, but I need you to give me an orgasm right now." Trust me, ladies your lover is up for the challenge. Women over forty ask how they are supposed to overcome the physical challenges of orgasming during pre-menopause or after menopause. Like everything in life, where there is a will, there is a way. Google hyaluronic acid topical and ingestible to start with...

Ask yourself right now. **How often do you allow your mind and body to be chemically balanced and happy like in the moments after orgasm?** Even if three a day is something you would never commit to, you should be striving for at least one a day. How can you compete in the workplace, have family harmony, and feel great about yourself at the level needed to do it all simultaneously if you are not treating your mind and body better than average?

Orgasms equal personal elation whether physical, mental or spiritual. By the same token, **sacrificing personal pleasure for work or family begins to drain your spirit.** And who doesn't love a good orgasm? The way you have an orgasm is up to you (with someone or alone doesn't matter) just make sure you have one daily – it's about the chemicals.

Would I have four children if I was orgasming daily? Would I have realized earlier that I was living a totally out-of-control existence? Would

I have changed anything? There are no answers to these questions. **The lesson is that you cannot concentrate on creating an amazing business and family life if you don't start by optimizing your own performance in every way.** So, put down the book for a moment and read the next chapter after you know what...

Chapter Fifteen

6570

Lesson Seventeen: Creating 'Sexy Opportunities'

Let's start this chapter backward with the lesson before learning the WHY behind it, shall we?

WE, female entrepreneurs of this world, are responsible for waking up every morning understanding that WE have the Brains, Boobs, and Balls to not only imagine, innovate, and execute our abundant futures but to further create massive opportunities for those around us. We ABSOLUTELY have the responsibility to consistently create opportunity for others.

It is my belief that entrepreneurs are merely opportunity creators that excel at bringing people together through ideas, passionate execution, and resources. I don't believe in hand-outs. I do believe in creating sexy opportunities for others, to take a hold of and accomplish something. For me, putting positive energy into the universe serves as a catalyst for fantastic action. I believe fantastic action as a result of sexy opportunity comes back to us 10X.

Consider some of the most incredible entrepreneurs of all time that give us proof of opportunity leading to fantastic action.

Steve Jobs changed the world forever with his invention of the iPod and iPhone. He donated over $50 million to Stanford hospitals and contributed to various projects to fight AIDS. As a philanthropist, Jobs' goal wasn't to be recognized, but to help those who needed it. His contributions to the hospital were opportunities for doctors and researchers to go beyond and create change in health care. Aside from his donations, he also provided countless others the opportunity to design and innovate in the emerging tech world that had not existed before.

Richard Branson, the famed Virgin billionaire entrepreneur, helped fund an organization called The Elders, comprised of a council of twelve elder statesmen such as Nelson Mandela, Kofi Annan, Jimmy Carter and Desmond Tutu who serve as "independent global leaders working together for peace and human rights." Imagine providing some of the greatest minds of our century the opportunity to carry on global conversations on current affairs.

Oprah Winfrey, in 2003, became the first African-American woman to reach billionaire status, according to *Forbes Magazine.* The Oprah Winfrey Foundation has contributed $10 million dollars to build and maintain the Oprah Winfrey Leadership Academy for Girls in South Africa. "Education is the way to move mountains, to build bridges, to change the world," she said. "Education is the path to the future. I believe that education is indeed freedom. With God's help, these girls will be the future leaders on the path to peace in South Africa and the world." She is providing the opportunity for these girls to become decision makers and leaders. This is only one of the many opportunities Oprah has created.

Melinda Gates was quoted as saying, "If you want to unlock the most progress for the most people, start by investing in women and girls." Since starting their namesake foundation in 1998, Melinda and Bill have committed more than $26 billion in grants providing vast opportunities.

CREATING OPPORTUNITY

In 2007, Sequoia Capital met with the co-founders of a new startup called Dropbox on the suggestion of a mutual friend. Drew Houston, one of the co-founders, showed off the storage software and painted his vision for the company. Eventually, this led to a financing round of $1.2 million that launched Dropbox as a full-fledged company. Would Dropbox be around today without this mutual friend and the opportunity he provided?

It's a good example of an opportunity presented and an opportunity seized. The friend provided the opportunity for the meeting, but it was Drew who made the opportunity go farther. Today, Dropbox remains one of the top websites consumers lists as one they would not want to lose. Good for Drew. Even better for the friend who was the catalyst for that opportunity and played a major role in how we entrepreneurs transfer information in this world.

When we focus on creating more value for other people, it completely shifts our perspective and makes us better, in business and at home. We will naturally start to move away from self-serving motives as we increasingly consider the welfare of others. Why? Our personal happiness and success become a byproduct of our efforts to contribute to the happiness and success of others. This kind of community consciousness elevates our existence to a much higher level. When we focus on adding value to the lives of others, it expands our world by multiples. It is then our responsibility to act on those opportunities to bring greater value into our lives so we can turn around and contribute to the success of others. It's a total win-win situation.

CREATING OPPORTUNITY IN DAY TO DAY BUSINESS

By developing your ability and consistency in creating opportunities you will build a stronger business. Here are some quick ideas to get you started

Make a daily connection call. Think about the universal karma you would create if you reached out to one person each day and asked them *"What are you working on today? Who could help you with that project or what resources do you need?"* Then sit back and listen. With an understanding of their needs, offer to help connect them to someone that can either solve their problem or help create an opportunity for them to get it solved. That person, delighted by the unsolicited help you offered, will now be inspired to reach out and do the same. Give help and get help. Your one phone call, the 15 minutes spared from your day, starts a chain of fantastic action.

Allow team members to sign up for a project outside their main area. There are plenty of projects that cut across lines of business, hierarchical levels, and functional specialties. Allow your team the chance to work on projects they are: a) not qualified to do; b) would never get to be a part of in their normal routine; c) allows them to work with mentors. The new skills, big-picture perspective, extra-group connections, and ideas about future projects can bring, are well worth the investment.

Before I started my own company, I was given the opportunity by my employer to create my first TV infomercial. He did not have to provide me this opportunity, and it was mine to squander potentially. Grateful for the opportunity, I made the most of it and produced a winner. He took a risk by giving a young employee so much room to play with his marketing budget, but he recognized he was giving me the chance to grow. Guess what. It paid off for him in a huge way and all these years later he is still profiting off of that commercial he gave me the opportunity to produce. Yes, this is the same boss that I quit on when he wouldn't give me a raise. In hindsight, it was the best scenario. **Expand your team's world of influence.** Look for opportunities outside your organization that allows team members to raise their profile. Create opportunities for them to teach, speak, or blog on topics relating to your business. Create opportunities for them to network regularly within and outside your industry. One of my examples came more than a dozen years ago when I "created the opportunity for" (read: forced) Jenn to attend a YPN event in the first few months after she joined the company. The opportunity I set up was for her to network with many different professionals in her new area, in and out of our industry, so that she could meet people but also establish her professional relationships. It was Jenn who seized this opportunity and met the man she would marry!

Create your opportunity from scratch. In the early 1990's, Joanne Chang graduated from Harvard and joined a prestigious management consulting firm. She hated it. Remembering she had a passion for cooking and was known as the "Chocolate Chip Cookie Girl" — she decided to give the restaurant world a try. "I sent a bunch of letters to chefs in town that I didn't know, but I knew their reputations," she says. "I wrote, 'I have no formal training, but I love cooking, and I'm interested in getting into the restaurant world, and I'll take any position.'" **BAM! That's fantastic action!**

Impressed with her initiative, intrigued by her resume, and short an employee who had just left, Boston power chef Lydia Shire called Joanne the next day. Chang started as "a bottom-of-the-ladder prep cook." Two decades later, Joanne is one of Boston's most celebrated restaurateurs.

Don't wait until you've 'made it' to start helping others, especially yourself. Your business and your personal life will grow 10X faster when you find ways to inspire action through opportunity.

LEVEL UP - CREATE SEXY OPPORTUNITIES

If you haven't guessed yet, I'm a big believer in 'SEX It Up' rather than 'Simplify It Down.' It's not sexual.

It is an attitude that says 'Others do ordinary. I do extraordinary. I put a little "extra" into my execution because you are worth it.'

In my experience, making something SEXY creates a specialness and memorability that helps everything take on a life of its own. For me, doing things simply is a way to disengage and get away with average.

As women, we tend to think simplicity leads to efficiency, control, and correctness. It is safe. We lead busy lives so why make things more complicated, right? Wrong!

Think about how you create opportunity in business, in your family and your bedroom. Is your thought process to make things simple and efficient or exciting and attractive?

You make things 'more complicated' because you are not striving for average - you have a personal brand as a mother, lover, and business leader that you have to uphold. You make it sexier because we only have

one life to live so why be boring about it – add some flare. Let me give you an example of creating Sexy Opportunity.

Cinderella's Corporate Give Back

As a Hispanic-American originally from Los Angeles, I'd always wanted a Quinceñera, one of the most important celebrations in my Mexican culture; a ceremony on a girl's fifteenth birthday with a wedding-like dress of bright colors and matching cake, to mark her passage to womanhood. Unfortunately, when my parents divorced it just wasn't possible. Years later, as I sat around the table with my girlfriends they joked about what I would do to celebrate my 40th birthday. I immediately told them that I was going to make them dress up in old prom dresses and be in my Quinceñera Court and go dancing at some night club. For months, our group joked about it, and as the months got closer, I began to post pictures of lavish Quinceñera dresses on my Facebook page asking them to choose their dresses for my upcoming birthday. And when I couldn't post any more dresses I put up pictures of lavish cakes. Then, videos of traditional Quinceñera dances. My girlfriends and I were having quite the time commenting back and forth. Then one day I get a private message from a girl I went to high school with who was now a 5th-grade teacher. She said she had been using my Facebook posts to teach the importance of culture in her mainly Hispanic classroom. Her student, Albert, had seen my posts and came up with this idea that he could design a dress for me to wear. I live in NJ. He lives in CA. We'd never met. The Universe presented me with the opportunity to give this boy a special moment in his life. I responded "yes, he could design the dress" and almost immediately I began getting pictures sent to me through Facebook of beautiful gowns he had drawn in class. He was quite talented.

Everyone is familiar with the story of the glass slipper that changed a young girl's life forever. I've always believed that the true magic was not in the glass slipper itself but rather the opportunity that the young girl was given by her Fairy Godmother to attend the Prince's Ball. It was this young girl's ability to turn the opportunity into her own happily ever after that has captured my entrepreneurial imagination since I can remember.

Like a true entrepreneur when presented with a new idea, the possibilities grew bigger and bigger – after all, the dress needed a place to be seen!

When I told my Synergixx team about the boy on Facebook, they were also inspired to turn this idea into a big opportunity for corporate 'Pay It Forward.' As with anything you add a little sexiness too – the opportunity took on a life of its own. Here are the facts:

- We created a 40th Birthday Gala in support of youth opportunity with a Cinderella theme including the big dresses, incredible cake, a live band, and other Latin fanfare/customs.
- We found a ballroom with the best views in Philadelphia to have a night of dinner and dancing.
- The dress would come to life the help of a local Philadelphia costume designer that would work with Albert via SKYPE. The dress was kept secret until the night of the event.
- We selected three charities that supported youth opportunity as special guests for the evening: Philadelphia's Covenant House for homeless teens, Open Hydrant Theatre Company in New York, which helps inner city kids using theater to get into college and on Broadway. And of course, iLEAD, the tuition-free project-based learning studio in California where Albert attends school.
- We then invited people to attend the Gala and, in lieu of birthday gifts, I asked for donations to the three charities.
- Albert and his teacher would be flown in for the event.
- The students from the theater group from New York would perform at the event.
- Teens from Philadelphia's Covenant House would also attend.
- A dance choreographed via Facebook for those attending (from all over the planet) to perform in unison during the evening without ever rehearsing together.
- The Synergixx Team was instructed to make it a night for all to remember.

Sounds like a pretty Sexy Opportunity, right?

At the time of writing this book, I have received more than twenty personal notes from women about what it meant to them to wear a ball gown. Each had their story, like never having a real wedding, or always being afraid to dress up and show off, or wanting to feel special after a terrible divorce. This Gala was giving them the opportunity to feel beautiful. The notes were incredibly inspiring.

The Gala was publicized so that people not attending could still support the charities. I began receiving emails from people I didn't know. One gentleman, so inspired by Albert's story of wanting to become a dress designer, wanted my permission to reach out the boy directly. The gentlemen was a clothing manufacturer from New York, who desired to mentor Albert after the event.

I received another email from a stranger not attending the Gala who was inspired by the story of the dress. He wanted not only to donate to the charities but asked me to help him create a similar event for one of his daughters who has just survived breast cancer at the age of thirty-four.

The night before the actual Gala, Albert was at my house and said to me, "If I become a dress designer one day, I want to…" I interrupted him.

"Albert, you are a dress designer already. You designed a dress and tomorrow I am going to wear it for the world to see. You have the opportunity to be an amazing dress designer for the rest of your life if you decide to keep drawing every day. How great of a dress designer you become is up to your hard work."

He stared back at me with a tiny smile spreading across his face. The light bulb went off. He had already achieved some level of his dream.

There are so many other opportunities that have come from this 40th birthday party idea that started between my girlfriends and me – too many to mention. The key here is that I only created the initial opportunity and the 'sexiness' drew people in, and the passion in the opportunity got them excited, and the excitement inspired them to create other opportunities. Where does it all end up? It will be years before we see the ripple effect but it is there.

Entrepreneurship. Becoming a parent. Cherishing a lover. Excelling as a businesswoman. All of it is about creating amazing moments for other people. In business. In family. In your personal world.

So, that was the lesson. As I promised, I'll end with how I learned to measure the importance of this lesson.

Life is not measured by the number of breaths we take, but by the moments that take our breath away.
—*Maya Angelou*

COMPILING THE NUMBERS

It's been eighteen years since I walked off that bridge holding my swollen breasts wrapped in duct tape. I've collected an incredible list of milestones since throwing the first punch on the bridge.

- Falling in love by 18
- Graduating college by 20
- Starting a new career by 21
- Delivering my first child by 24
- Becoming an entrepreneur by 24
- Generating $5M in sales by 27
- Delivering my second child by 27
- Writing my first book at 28
- Losing both my parents by 29
- Delivering my third child by 29
- Generating $17M in sales by 29
- Becoming a radio show host by 30
- Producing three rap music videos by 31
- Becoming a TV host by 31
- Being diagnosed with a disease at 33
- Starting my second company at 35
- Writing my second book by 35
- Starting my third company at 35
- Co-writing my third book at 36
- Starting two podcasts at 36
- Almost going bankrupt by 36

- Growing my company to new levels of profitability at 37
- And the list continues still

Measuring the Moments

I've been traveling on this road for eighteen years as an entrepreneur, as a woman-in-training, and thinking 'what am I doing here?' I've spent 365 days of each one of these years as a mom and a wife desperately trying to get it all right. That's a total of 6570 days over those 18 years that has lead me far enough down the road to becoming a proud mother, grateful wife, happy woman, and enlightened entrepreneur. Today, numbers no longer mean anything to me.

Moments mean everything. I became an entrepreneur to live life on my terms and create my destiny. **Somewhere along the way, life became a job not a passion.** The monetary, judgmental record keeping of the numbers in my reality became more important and quantifiable than the number of inspiring moments I created or experienced. I became relentless in the pursuit of never giving up. But I was missing the moments that made hanging in there worth it.

It took my six-year-old daughter to point out that I was not relentless in my self-expectations for all that is worthwhile in life. It took her eyes to make me see that being relentless in creating and savoring memorable moments was the only important achievement in any one of my roles. I'm not apologizing for my journey. It all makes sense to me now. It has forged who I am. It has made me secure in how I continue on this road. I'm thriving in mind, body and spirit as a result. I'm finally able to enjoy my success while still being fearless in my pursuit for more.

Brains. Boobs. Balls. I got it all together now. YES! Every day there is something that threatens to collapse my world. Struggles never end. Yet I'm peaceful. **Today, I passionately choose moments over numbers.**

It's the moments I'm collecting now and moments I'm committed to creating for others. Moments of great pleasure, passion, promise, and opportunity. I'm on a new road now.

I want to create 6570 amazing, life-altering moments for other people before I turn fifty. It means I have 365 days a year, for the next decade, to create these moments – that's only 18 opportunities I have to create in each day if I start right now. It feels like a great Core Driver to add to my list for this new decade I'm entering.

What will my world look like as Mother, Wife, and Entrepreneur after I've created these 6570 amazing moments for myself and others in the world? I can't wait to find out.

6570
Isn't it funny how the numbers add up?

Special Thank You to My Support Family

Jenn Nading – Thank you for believing in me when every bone in your body told you not to.

TJ Muldoon – Thank you for always being on my side through this wild ride and being my partner in "we'll make it work."

Aunt Rose – Thank you for being my partner in 'many crimes'.

Tony and Cindy Fusco – Thank you for being the best friend-parents this orphan girl could ask for.

Team Synergixx – you made me the Entrepreneur/CEO I am today. Thank you for allowing me to be a work in progress.

My Circle of Chicks – thank you Shemina Gheewalla, Michele Peraino, Karen Ognibene, Kim Bersani and Kathy Murphy for letting me be a girlfriend – nothing more or less. So important to my success.

Ms. Hall – Thank you for burying my short-shorts deep in that timecapsule and telling me you expected more from me. It made the biggest difference.

Mrs. Rosenberg (Rosie) – for teaching me that rehearsal always outweighs raw talent.

George Faltaous —my brother in business - we are the most unlikely of siblings, and I have learned tremendously from you.

Maria Watson – Thank you for being my first female mentor in business, relentless in your desire to see me succeed, and opening me up to our very special friendship.

Evan Morgenstein – Thank you reminding me that allowing yourself to trust someone you barely know can create the most amazing magic. I'm ready to take uncomfortable entrepreneurial action – again – because of our friendship.

And to the countless people who told me it couldn't be done. Perhaps you were my most productive inspirations!